Life's Journey our Greatest Test

A Contemporary Christian Novel

MARSHALEE PATTERSON

Copyright © 2021 Marshalee Patterson

All rights reserved.

No part of this book may be reproduced or transmitted in any form, without the prior written approval of the author.

This is a work of fiction but with real-life experiences. Most of the places mentioned in the book are fictional except for the different states, but all the characters are entirely fictitious and are drawn totally from the author's imagination. Any resemblance to persons living or dead is purely coincidental

ISBN-13: 9798476030584

DEDICATION

I dedicate this book to my deceased husband, Jeffrey Melna, who inspired the first half of the main character's life. This goes out to every person who thought that they were or still are alone while facing life's trials such as interfamilial rape that makes us feel ashamed, and bad habits such as developing drug addiction when trying to cope with the death of a loved one, which leads us down a negative path.

The Bible itself tells us that the same sufferings we face are also experienced by our brothers across the world. I believe that was to show us we are not alone in our sufferings. I leave this verse of encouragement with you all. The Lord sent me this message when I wanted to give up on his greatest gift to me, which I had been fasting for many months beforehand.

Hebrew 12:2 says, looking to Jesus, the author, and finisher of our faith, who for the joy that was set before Him endured the cross, despising the shame and has sat down at the right hand of the throne of God. Be of good courage and let the Lord strengthen your hearts. Amen.

Lots of love,

CONTENTS

	Acknowledgements	i
1	Freedom	1
2	A New Day Dawning	Pg #11
3	Reminiscing	Pg #18
4	New Acquaintances	Pg #24
5	Grandma's Ruth Farewell Gift	Pg #31
6	Taking a Chance	Pg #37
7	A Fresh Start	Pg #46
8	Discovering Life Again	Pg#54
9	Digging up old Wounds	Pg #61
10	A Very Dark Period	Pg #65
11	Threading Unknown Waters	Pg #72
12	A Moment of Gratitude	Pg #79
13	Facing My Demons	Pg #85
14	Brady and his Dad	Pg #93
15	Venting out Frustrations	Pg #100
16	Birds of a Feather	Pg #107

17	Life at St. Peter's	Pg #117
18	Survival	Pg#129
19	Making Amends	Pg #140
20	Breaking Bad Habits for Good	Pg #149
21	Coming to Terms with the Past	Pg #163
22	Hitting Rock Bottom	Pg #174
23	Getting Acquainted	Pg #180
24	Discovering Lexington and Getting Busted	Pg #190
25	An Overdue Reunion	Pg #201
26	Restoration and Deeper Connection	Pg#209
27	Bittersweet Goodbyes	Pg #216
28	Happy Times	Pg #221
29	A Stranger's Homecoming	Pg #229
30	Impulsive Clara	Pg #234
31	The Mystery	Pg #241
32	Solving the Mystery	Pg #247
33	Renewed Friendship	Pg #255
34	Wedding Preparations	Pg #260
35	Surprise!	Pg #268

36	Shawn and Clara	Pg #277
37	Shawn on the Battle Field	Pg#285
38	Celebration Time	Pg #293
39	Newlyweds	Pg #302
40	A Silver Lining Emerged	Pg #308
41	Passing the Test	Pg #317
	Word from the Author	Pg#323
	Other Books by the Author	Pg #324
	Sinner's Prayer	Pg #326
	About the Author	Pg #328

ACKNOWLEDGEMENTS

I want to thank Samantha Pico for assisting with editing this manuscript. The Holy Spirit who guided me in writing this book, which was not easy to bring to light with all the traumatic experiences of the characters.

For I know the thoughts that I have towards you, saith the Lord, thoughts of peace and not of evil, to give you an expected end. (Jeremiah 29:11)

CHAPTER 1- FREEDOM

Brady O'Connor stood outside the Lexington Prison's entrance and stared at the fortress that influenced his life's perspective. His time inside also helped him turn away from the destructive path on which he was.

To many who had heard of Lexington Prison, it brought chills to their spines, and for others, the very thought of going there kept them on the straight and narrow. A mere passerby walking alongside the walls of Lexington Prison would not get the impression of it being a terrible place.

But like many things in life, where the outer appearance often deceives many, so did Lexington. The walls stood majestic and tall. They glowed with a radiant reddish-brown. On top of its perimeter walls was barbed wire, which infused security in passersby, leaving the prisoners incapable of escaping and troubling society.

Brady turned his back towards the prison's entrance and looked out onto the busy street, watching the vehicles as they passed one by one.

He had no idea what he was to do with his life now.

Throwing his duffle bag over his shoulder, he flagged down an approaching bus. The bus stopped a few paces from him at what seemed to be the designated stop, causing him to chase after it. Once he paid his fare, he strolled past the few passengers and sat at the back of the bus. He leant back against the seat and closed his eyes. Thoughts of his grandmother, Ruth, popped into his head. He smiled.

Ruth had always believed a lot of good was inside the darkened shell of a man he had been. She would always encourage him and often used Bible verses to convey her messages of hope to show him that God, the Father, was never far from him, even in the darkness that had surrounded him.

Brady loved her and always listened to her, even if he could not understand her faithful devotion to God, who he thought had failed him the day his brother, John, died. In Ruth's last letter, she had not informed him of her illness or that she was nearing death. Her words were only of encouragement and about the painting he created for her when he was fourteen.

Brady, she wrote, *God has, indeed, blessed you with a special gift, and looking at this painting, I can see the man whom He called you to be. Sometimes it seems I can feel His presence more when I'm looking at your painting. There is such a light in you that I don't ever want to see go out. And, for that reason, I haven't stopped praying for God to deliver you from all your troubles. Take heart, my dear; the eyes of the Lord are always upon the righteous, and His ears are open to their cry. Trust in Him always.*

A few teardrops slipped from Brady's eyes. He averted his gaze to the window to escape the passengers' glares, who would often glance in his direction after seeing him get on at Lexington Prison. The journey to Ruth's house was exactly twenty-five hours after transferring to a Greyhound bus, with three bus transfers.

His muscles ached, and the long drive made him anxious. Nonetheless, he smiled in appreciation for the scenic view, which relaxed his mind for most of the journey. He felt pleased about being one of the last passengers to disembark the bus that he turned to face the driver once he disembarked.

"Thank you, Sir, for a pleasant drive." He smiled with a slight nod. "Have a good night."

The driver reciprocated by tipping his hat, "You, too, young man." He then closed the bus door and drove out of sight.

Brady took a deep breath. The walk towards Ruth's house would take him off the main road and onto a quiet, little track that snaked through the wooded area of Memphis, Tennessee's countryside. After walking for a couple of minutes, he pulled his hoodie over his head to protect his cheeks from the chill in the air. He stopped and smiled. Memories of when he and

John used to run through the woods, playing hide and seek in the trees and playing cowboy and Indians surfaced.

Flickering lights from the neighbouring houses switched his thoughts to that of the last letter he had received. Mrs. Walsh, his grandmother's best friend, and a next-door neighbour had informed him of Ruth's passing and of what she had left him.

As he approached the front door to Mrs. Walsh's house, Brady wondered if her granddaughter, Clara, still lived there. Clara had been a friend of his and John's since they had visited their grandmother as kids. A sudden nervousness overcame him as he knocked on the door.

He pondered what she would think of him, knowing he'd been locked up in Lexington Prison for the past seven years, knowing that only the most unpredictable of criminals ended up there. He felt the shame of it taking hold of him. He shook himself as to not entertain any negative thoughts.

She might understand, like Gram, he thought, trying to reassure himself.

A few minutes passed before the door opened, revealing a petite Asian woman. Wrinkles and a bright smile creased her face.

"Brady!" Without warning, the old woman, who stood a little shorter than him, pulled him into a tight embrace. "How are you?" she asked softly after she released him. She stared up at him.

Brady smiled back at her, "I'm okay, Mrs. Walsh."

"Well, then, good." She looped her arm through his. "Come, let's go inside, and I'll make you something to eat. I know you must be hungry after such a long journey."

"I certainly am," he chuckled and walked with her into the house.

Upon entering the living room, Mrs. Walsh pointed to the couch and said, "Have a seat, Brady; be back in a few minutes."

With short, quick steps, Mrs. Walsh darted across the room and disappeared into the kitchen. Brady let out a long breath and removed his duffle bag from his shoulders. He dropped it on the couch, sank next to it, and leant back. Closing his eyes, he smiled and thought of pleasant times he had spent in this house with Clara and John.

"Here you go," Mrs. Walsh said a few minutes later, breaking his trip down memory lane. She placed a tray on the coffee table in front of him.

Brady opened his eyes and smiled. "Thank you."

"You're welcome, my dear." Mrs. Walsh pulled up her favourite chair next to the couch and sat down. She smiled, watching Brady as he closed his eyes and said a quick prayer over his food. "There's more if you want," she added when he opened his eyes and reached for the chicken sandwich.

Brady nodded. By the time he finished swallowing the last of the chicken sandwich, he had turned to look at Mrs. Walsh for the first time since he started eating. "That tasted so good, Mrs. Walsh. Thank you." He reached for the cup of hot chocolate, closed his eyes, and savoured the taste while he sipped. "I needed this."

Mrs. Walsh chuckled. "Oh! Before I forget, Brady, let me get that envelope your grandmother left for you." She leapt to her feet and scurried from the room.

Brady picked up the tray containing the cup and dish and sauntered into the kitchen. He placed them in the sink and proceeded to wash them. A radiant smile covered his face as more memories of himself, John, and Clara flooded his mind. He thought about them running in and out of this very kitchen to sample Mrs. Walsh's baked goods that comprised great cakes and pies.

It was an old fashion house; lots of green shrubberies ran along its walls, as was the case in most houses in the area. Like all the people in this wooded region, Mrs. Walsh kept most of her windows closed throughout the daytime to keep lizards and other small creatures out of the house.

The kitchen area was spacious and never put Brady, Clara, or John at any risk of getting hurt while Mrs. Walsh baked. The backyard, however, was small, but this did not put a damper on them having fun since they utilised the woods and the river most.

"Oh, Brady, you didn't need to wash those. You're my guest," Mrs. Walsh said, startling him as she entered the kitchen and saw him placing the plate in the dish drainer.

Brady dried his hands on the dishtowel that hung in front of the sink. Then he turned around as she approached him and leaned back against the sink.

"Mrs. Walsh, you're not a stranger to me, although it's been a while since I last saw you. But I'd feel awful just eating your food and not helping you at least clean up. You're not so young anymore either," he teased with a smirk on his face.

She chuckled at his remark and stretched the envelope to him. "Here you go."

Brady reached for the envelope and stared at it, almost as if he was afraid to open it.

"It's the deed to the house, the keys, and a bank book with your name in it. Ruth loved you very much, Brady. She left her life savings in that account. It's not millions, but enough to help you start something new with your life. Sometimes she and I would sit out on the porch, and she would ask me to pray with her for you. One thing she always asked God for was to bring you to the light that He brought out of you through your paintings when you were a boy," Mrs. Walsh informed him with a gentle pat on the shoulder. "Oh, hold on, Brady!"

Mrs. Walsh took a closer step to the sink and pulled open one of its drawers. After shuffling through all its contents, she pulled out a flashlight and tested to see if it worked. Feeling satisfied, she shoved the drawer closed, then stretched the flashlight to Brady.

"What's this for?" he questioned her, confused.

"You'll need it on your way over. Ruth had asked me to disconnect all the utilities after she died. She did not want the money she left you to be eaten up by bills since no one would be living there other than yourself. You'll need to go into town to get them reconnected."

"Oh, okay, thanks." He took the flashlight from her hands and stepped away from the sink. "I better be heading over now, too."

"Alright, let me walk you to the door." Mrs. Walsh stepped ahead of him and led the way.

Upon entering the living room, Brady stopped by the couch, tucked the flashlight under his arm, and reached for his duffle bag.

"Hold on, Mrs. Walsh," he called after her when she almost made it to the door to the hallway.

She spun around a bit fast, thinking something was wrong, and then chuckled to herself when she saw Brady loosening the drawstring of his bag and thrusting the envelope inside. When he closed the bag and proceeded to put it on his back, she spoke.

"Brady, I want you to have dinner with me in the evenings. I don't want you to be too alone all day, and I could use the company myself, too," she smiled.

"I would like that, too, Mrs. Walsh." He took a few quick strides towards her. When he neared her, he kissed her cheek and smiled. "Thank you for always being so kind."

A big smile spread across her face. "You've made an old woman happy." She looped her arm through his as they proceeded to the front door.

"Has much changed in town since I last visited?" Brady asked while Mrs. Walsh pulled back the locks on the door.

"Not so much, just a few new businesses."

Mrs. Walsh pushed the door open, then

turned to Brady, "I'm glad your home."

"Thank you so much, Mrs. Walsh, for everything you gave me tonight. I needed it. For so many years, I felt lost, even from myself, but Gram kept seeing a light in me that I could not recognise. I can't change all the terrible things I did, but I've asked God every day to help me get past the nightmare of it all and to help me walk in His light. I also want to make Gram proud."

"Don't feel too bad. We all do terrible things in life that we later regret. Some more than others, but that does not mean the one who does less is loved any more than the one who does a lot in the eyes of God, our Father. To Him, we all need his love equally. Sometimes even the sin that does not seem to do much damage on the surface is causing far worst beneath. You're only twenty-nine, Brady. Embrace your second chance."

He smiled and nodded in agreement. Just as he stepped outside, he turned to face her. "Mrs. Walsh, I had wanted to ask you from the minute you opened your door—about Clara—but when you hugged me, everything slipped my mind. Where is she now, and how is she doing?"

"Ah, my dear, she went off to join her parents in Canada eight years ago. She's a nurse now." Mrs. Walsh smiled and then continued. "She almost got married two years ago but called it off without any explanation to anyone." Her brows furrowed in perplexity. "Whatever happened—only she and her ex-fiancé know."

"Does she know about . . . . . . about me?" he asked nervously.

"Yes, she does. And don't worry; she doesn't

hate you. Although, she hated how you let your life go down that destructive pathway."

"Thanks again, Mrs. Walsh—goodnight."

"Goodnight, Brady. Remember to stop by tomorrow for dinner."

"I will."

As Brady walked off into the dark, his mind wandered to Clara again.

Oh, Clara, what kind of secret are you keeping from everyone?

CHAPTER 2- A NEW DAY DAWNING

By the time Brady arrived at the front door to his grandmother's house, it was almost 8 p.m. and very dark. The flashlight Mrs. Walsh had loaned him proved to be a lifesaver, sparing him from tumbling. Once inside, he marched straight into the kitchen and rummaged for matches in cupboards and drawers.

Soon, his lips curled into a smile when he pulled a full pack from the back of the utensil drawer. He tucked it away into his jacket pocket, then pondered for a moment to remember where his grandmother kept her emergency lamps.

With careful steps, he climbed the stairs and walked into his and John's old bedroom. He strolled over to the window and carelessly dropped his duffle bag on the chair that leant against the wall. He stared outside. Everything was in outer darkness. The only gleam of light came from the moon that sparkled against the Wolf River. Although the river stood a little distance from the house, his room had a great view of it.

A few minutes passed before he stepped away from the window and shone the flashlight on the dresser. A smile spread across his face when he spotted a medium-sized lamp sitting on top of it, and he scampered towards it. *Ah*, the lamp still contained just enough oil to last through the night. He laid the flashlight next to the lamp and withdrew the pack of matches from his pocket. A gush of cool air blew into the room as he removed the lamp shade.

Quickly, he lit the lantern then walked back over to the window to close the latch. The river called to him, which caused him to stare at it. It was the place he always found refuge when he wanted to be alone. An urge to take a shower rushed through his body after looking at its shimmering, moonlit water. He picked up the flashlight and turned his heels to the bedroom's bathroom. A groan escaped his lips as he turned the shower knob, remembering the water had been disconnected.

"First thing tomorrow morning," he mumbled.

Brady switched off the flashlight as he walked back into the bedroom and towards the bed. He sank onto the mattress and exhaled, then he laid the flashlight on the nightstand. Leaning forward, he loosened the laces of his boots before kicking them off his feet. He pushed them under his bed—something he always did while in Lexington. With a swift flick of his wrist, he pulled the covers aside, slipped beneath them, and closed his eyes.

The first night on a soft, warm bed helped him to sleep right through the night. His Lexington routine, however, caused him to wake up early the next day. With heavy eyes, Brady glanced at the bedside clock and saw it flashing 7:00 a.m.

Adjusting the covers, he rolled onto his other side and drifted off again. A bright light illuminated the room. He opened his eyes again. This time, when he looked over at the clock, it blinked five past one.

Brady sat up in bed and took a deep breath.

"What now?" he asked himself.

Thoughts of what Mrs. Walsh told him about the utilities popped in his mind, and he groaned. He had no desire to go into town and be around anyone—not yet. He tried to rationalise that he was used to the dark from his days in solitary at Lexington, and the Wolf River was nearby for him to shower when needed to.

Rising to his feet, he walked across the room and reached for his duffle bag to retrieve his toothbrush. He remembered that he had no toothpaste or soap.

Nonetheless, he smiled, knowing his grandmother always thought of everything. He walked into the bathroom and opened the cabinet to check if she had Mrs. Walsh buy him toiletries. Only half a bar of soap sat in the cabinet.

"I guess I have to go to town after all. I need to hurry if I want to try getting any of these utilities on today," he sighed.

In the bedroom, he pulled out a pair of jeans, underwear and a white T-shirt from the bag, tucked them under his arm, and then headed off to the river.

The water felt so therapeutic against his skin. Oh, how he needed it. The smell of fresh water out in its natural surrounding relaxed him. He almost did not want to get out. *I must come back here later and do this again*, he thought to himself.

After spending about fifteen minutes swimming around, he got out and hurried back to the house. He picked up all the documents he needed and rushed off to catch the bus going into town.

Twenty-five minutes later, he arrived in town and walked into the bank. Although no one there knew of his past, he felt very self-conscious from the looks he received. It was as if voices of condemnation shouted at him. He froze where he stood inside the bank, unable to move.

"Are you okay, Sir? You look pale. Can I offer you some assistance?" the voice of a middle-aged woman asked, pulling him from his state of fright.

Brady inhaled before he turned and looked at her from head-to-toe. He then smiled in relief when he realised he was only having a nervous moment.

"Oh, . . . yes, I'm all right. Thank you for your concern, ma'am," he explained. "My name is Brady O'Connor. My grandmother opened an account here for me, and I need access to it. Is that something you can assist me with?" he asked, remembering his reason for being there.

"Well, that's not my department, but I can show you someone who can," she said, smiling. "Follow me this way."

The woman led him over to a customer service agent and explained the situation to the young woman sitting at the desk before she faced him again. "Have a good day, Mr. O'Connor."

"Thank you for your help."

Everything went smoothly from there, and after twenty-five minutes, Brady walked out of the bank. Upon arriving at the electric company, he groaned aloud when he opened the door and saw the large crowd standing inside.

Why don't people pay their bills on time instead of rushing to do so at the last minute? This causes so much chaos. He thought to himself while pushing his way through the crowd towards the customer service desk.

Thirty-five minutes of standing in the customer service line had Brady rotating his shoulders to relieve the tension. He sighed in relief when he saw the monitor blinking his number and briskly marched towards the counter.

"Here's the amount you need to pay to have the service reconnected, Mr. O'Connor. You will have your light back on two hours after you've made your payment," the straight-faced agent informed. She then turned his attention towards the payment line, and with a sympathetic smile, she pointed. "That's the line you will need to join to make your payment, Mr. O'Connor. Enjoy the rest of your day," she added.

"Thank you."

An hour and a half later, Brady walked out

of the electricity company, annoyed. He had no idea he would have stood that long in one line, waiting to pay a bill.

"Great," he grumbled, looking at the closed sign on the water company's door. Although he felt disappointed, his stomach growled, redirecting his attention to food.

Brady sat in a diner and stared through the window; everything looked so foreign to him. He recognised no one, though it had been ten years since he had last been in this town. He thought he may have seen at least one person he knew. After paying his bill, he walked out and headed to the supermarket to purchase his groceries and toiletries before he headed back home.

When he opened the front door, he flipped the light switch to see if the light company had fulfilled their promise and smiled when he saw they had. He packed the groceries away in the kitchen and ran upstairs to put the toiletries away in his bathroom.

Up until this point, he had not looked around the house as of yet, but after he left his room and headed back down the stairs, he noticed the photos hanging on the walls, most of which were of him. They brought a smile to his face. When he entered the living room, sadness crept upon him when he saw the family photos.

His grandmother loved keeping memories of everyone. He saw his parents' wedding photo—how happy they were. Both his parents were of Irish descent and college sweethearts. They had promised each other that they would get married right after graduation. They were so much in love with each other.

His eyes then shifted to the other photos standing next to that of his parents. He chuckled at the one of himself and John getting ice cream cones from their grandmother when they visited the fair. There were also photos of him and John in their baseball uniforms back in junior high, fishing together with their dad, and even one of him, John, and Clara swimming down by the river. Ruth's photos showed how close they were all their lives.

Brady and John were only a year apart, with John the oldest of the two. One picture, however, caused Brady to lose his composure after seeing it. It was the one John took just before he was to go off to the Navy.

Brady smiled, remembering how proud he felt to have a brave brother who wanted to fight for their country. He also remembered how excited John was to know he would be joining him in a year. Brady pulled the photo to his chest, then walked over to the sofa and sat down. He closed his eyes and squeezed them tight to suppress the tears that threatened to fall.

A frightened eighteen-year-old drug addict had robbed his brother of his future and his life. All because John was trying to help him make the right decision to go to the police station and sort out whatever mess he had found himself in with the police. It only caused the kid to panic and tried to flee, and in his frenzy, he stabbed John.

By the time Brady and his mum, Claudette, arrived at the hospital, it was just in time to see them pulling the sheet over John's head.

CHAPTER 3- REMINISCING

"John, you being the hero that you were caused you to be taken from me. My life would have been so different today if you were still here. We both could have been naval captains by now, happily married with kids of our own," Brady said, staring at the photo he held.

Tears cascaded down his face without control as he reflected on that difficult time. The memory was still so fresh in his mind. Though the cops brought John to the emergency room shortly after the stabbing, it still did not aid in stopping the bleeding. The puncture wound had proven lethal.

Upon learning the details of John's death from the doctor in charge, who had done his best to save John, he and his mum sat, horrified in the hospital's waiting area, unable to accept it. Everything the doctor said thereafter fell on deaf ears, even his condolences. It took a gentle shake from the doctor to get his attention.

"Is there someone I can call? I don't think it's wise to let you both go home alone in the state you're currently in," the doctor had asked.

"You can call my dad, Frank O'Connor. He lives in Lancaster, Pennsylvania with his new wife now, but he'll come," Brady remembered, telling the doctor.

That was the first time he had seen his dad shed tears. Frank was the type of man who hid his pain well. Throughout the twelve years of his parents' marriage, Brady could recall the many occasions his father would call him and John "sissy boys" when he saw them crying.

He would say that once a boy passed the age of five, his tears should stop. Denise, Frank's new wife, had helped with the funeral arrangements and also in consoling Claudette, who had clammed up until she saw John's coffin lower into the ground.

It was Denise who encouraged Claudette to be strong for her surviving son, for whom she should show optimism and help him come to terms with the loss. That was when his mum returned to her old self.

Remorse coursed through Brady's body as he sat on the sofa. When Frank and Denise left Philadelphia and went back to Lancaster to resume their lives, his mum, Claudette, had a hard time getting him to focus on his studies when he resumed classes. He had taken John's death hard and caused his mum even more grief due to the numerous phone calls from his school: his fight breakouts and outright disrespect to his teachers.

Brady knew back then he did not make it easy for his mother. Even though he knew she was hurting as well, he didn't care at that time. Everyone enraged him. His otherwise caring personality changed after his brother's death; his brother was too concerned for others. To Brady, no one else mattered but himself.

As he sat, reflecting on that time in his life, the realisation of how hard it was for his mum to watch him self-destruct turned his remorse to anger. She had often tried to sit him down at home and talk to him about his attitude, even mentioning that John would not have wanted to see him acting the way he did. That was the only way she got through to him.

"I'm sorry, Mum." Brady wiped away whatever visible trace of tears from his face and took a deep breath. "I know you tried your best to help me cope, and I wanted so much to be there for you, but I just couldn't accept that John, who was so good to everyone, was gone and never coming back."

He took a glance around the living room with a long exhale. He felt worn out from such melancholic memories, and it had been a long day. Brady dragged himself up from the sofa to replace the photo beside the others. He stepped out of the living room and trudged up the stairs to his bedroom.

The next morning, he awoke at 7:00 a.m. again. *Seems it will take some time before my body gets used to being out of Lexington.* Brady reached for the alarm clock and set it to go off at 9:00 a.m., then pulled the covers over his head and drifted off back to sleep. When he woke later, he felt more refreshed than the previous day.

"I can go to the water company today at about noon, seeing I don't have to rush off to town as I did yesterday—*but* only after I take a good, long swim in the river." He smiled to himself as he descended the stairs on his way to the kitchen to prepare his breakfast.

Brady lifted the cheese and tomato omelette from the frying pan, placed it on his plate, and then poured himself a cup of steaming hot coffee. As he strolled to the table, his mind drifted back to breakfast time at Lexington, which was usually very meagre.

He smiled to himself, thanking God that since he was a boy, he never felt the need to overindulge in having a large breakfast. His control when abundance was around kept him through those days at Lexington. After placing his coffee and omelette onto the table, he pulled back his chair, sat down, and closed his eyes.

"Thank you, Lord, for what you have provided for me today. Teach me how to walk in your way and guide me throughout this day in Jesus's name. Amen."

He formed the habit of praying before he ate, after finally letting God have his way in his life. Being in Lexington that final year, he saw change in himself. His grandmother's prayers for him had begun to take effect. He was calmer and more hospitable to the other prisoners, some of whom had grown fearful of him. Somehow, he could never figure out the origin of the level of rage, which he had developed.

After breakfast, as he walked along the dirt

track behind his backyard down to the river, he could not help but smile, appreciating the blessings of nature and the freedom to embrace it. Brady jumped into the clear, blue water and laughed aloud, feeling renewed. He swam back and forth, relaxing and freeing his mind from all the past.

After about an hour, he got out and dressed, walked back to the house, and picked up the documents needed. He headed to town. It was 12:30 p.m. when he walked into the water company, Water Works.

Unlike the previous day, there were not as many customers inside. The customer service desk had only one person before him. Within a few minutes, he got the information needed and was directed to a line to pay his reconnection fee, which he calculated had about twenty customers in total. He smiled, thinking he would be out the door within the next forty-five minutes or less, but soon, he grew disgruntled when he saw how slow the agents worked.

He tried to keep his composure and not yell at the agents to move faster. It was the thought of how much he needed the water connected that kept him waiting a full hour before his paperwork was processed.

When he stepped outside Water Works, he raised the envelope containing all his documents over his eyes to shield them from the sun's glare. Having no urgent place to be or any pressing matters to tend to, he began to stroll through the town at a leisurely pace. He looked around to see if there was anyone he would recognise and observe how much the town had changed.

Most of the places in town were the same, except for a few new shops and a new, tall building that looked like a corporate company. No face seemed familiar.

Well, it's probably for the best. Maybe now I can start fresh, having nothing from my past to haunt me, he thought.

As Brady continued walking, he soon noticed a partially burnt, abandoned building. It looked like a factory—from the sign attached to the surrounding fence.

After noticing there weren't any *'no trespassing'* signs, he lifted the very thick, dirty chain on the closed gates high above his head, as not to soil his shirt. He slipped underneath and began nosing around the compound. As hard as he tried, he could not remember which factory it was that once stood there; not that this street was one he had often travelled when he visited his grandmother.

Once inside the building, he held a firm grip on the railing of what was once a wide staircase as he climbed the steps. He could see traces of baby blue on the blackened wall due to the fire. As he got to the top of the stairs, he felt like a victim in a slasher film.

CHAPTER 4- NEW ACQUAINTANCES

Chills ran along his spine as he ambled along the corridor of the factory's second floor. Ghastly whispers now filled his ears, with nothing in sight to connect to the strange sounds. Brady wondered if the ghosts of his past had returned to rob him of the new beginning he so longed for.

As he continued walking, the urge to turn back shot through him, but his legs would not cooperate with his brain. He froze at the sound of a terrible cough that echoed across the hallway. His heart pounded hard in his chest, and his breathing intensified as he tried to distinguish whether it was human. His eyes darted from left to right, trying to figure out from which room the sound emanated.

Snap out of it! How can you be fearful, for a man who isn't afraid of anyone and even once didn't care about anything? Even worse, you now call yourself a born-again Christian, and you are letting fear grip you. Get a hold of yourself! Remember, God's word says: he does not give us a spirit of fear, but of power, love, and a sound mind, he internalised, trying to encourage himself.

Brady shook himself and focused on where the sound resonated the loudest. He stepped into the second room to his right. From where he stood, papers and foliage scattered across the empty room. Sunlight permeated into the room from what remained of a burnt-out medium-sized window.

A slight movement among a bundle of papers at the far end corner of the room caught his attention. He gasped when he saw the figure of a person. With slow, careful steps, he moved forward, curious to see what manner of person would hide away in such a place like this. His eyes dilated when those of a frightened young woman stared back at him.

"Hey, . . . I'm not going to hurt you," Brady told her in a gentle voice.

Her gaze remained fixated on him, watching his every movement while she clung to the wall like a security blanket. Brady stooped down, facing her, maintaining eye contact with her. He empathised with her, knowing what he himself had gone through. He wanted to help her—but would she let him?

This may be my opportunity to do something good for someone, to prove to God that I am worthy of the second chance I so craved, he thought.

"*Please* . . . I know I don't know you, but

please let me help you somehow. I know what being homeless is like, hiding away from the world. But the dangers of living on the streets landed me in prison, from where I came only a few days ago. I'm trying to start over, and, even now, I'm still having a hard time getting over the pain I've caused my family."

He choked on his words. He didn't know why he shared that with this stranger but felt opening up would allow her to see she was not alone in suffering hardships. He hoped it would allow her to at least give him a chance to help her.

"My name is Brady; I live at Glen-Close Avenue two miles from here. It is very beautiful and peaceful there. I know I cannot ask you to trust me, as I am a stranger to you, but I have an extra room you could stay in if you want to. This is not a place for a young woman to be. If you need time to trust in my sincerity, at least allow me to bring you some food here each day," he said, hoping she would give him the chance to feed her.

She stared into his green eyes and saw a gleam of kindness but kept her guard up. "I'm Sara. Thank you," she whispered in her protective, seated position.

"Nice to meet you, Sara," Brady smiled gratefully. "Are you hungry? I could get you something to eat before I head back home today."

"Yea . . . ssss," she stuttered and nodded her head.

"I'll be back in a few minutes. *Please* don't disappear—just let me help you."

As Brady scurried down the factory's steps,

he wondered if it all had been a dream. He picked up his pace once he got through the gates of the factory and didn't stop until he stood outside the doors of the food court, trying to catch his breath.

"Please, Lord, give me the chance to help this lady. Let her come to trust in my sincerity. Let her not be gone when I return."

On his way back to the factory, he kept hoping that God had granted him his request. He ran up the stairs and almost slipped, anxious to see if she waited. His heart sank the minute he walked back into the room where he left her. She was nowhere in sight.

Brady felt his one opportunity to do right for another was lost. He fell back against the wall and sank to the floor. He placed the food beside him on the floor, pulled his knees up to his face, and wrapped his arms around them. Then he lowered his head and wept.

He felt hopeless.

A few minutes later, the sounds of paper crushing caused him to lift his head. Sara was back in her corner. He smiled in relief.

"I thought you had vanished. Where did you go?"

"I had to pee, and I had to go outside to the back of the building," she replied, still suspicious of his intentions.

"Can I ask you what caused you to be out here by yourself?"

She shook her head nervously, "Not yet."

Brady surmised something or someone must have scared her and caused her to be afraid to trust others. He hoped with time, she would come to trust him. "Here's the food," he stretched the paper bag with the meal and drink inside towards her.

Sara glanced at the food with suspicion, causing him to chuckle.

"Okay, I understand." Brady pulled back the bag towards him and withdrew the food. He took a small piece of chicken from the box, bit into it, and took a sip from the drink before handing them to her again. This time, she took them from his hands.

Brady sat with her and watched her while she ate. His mind was soon flooded with questions about her: *whether she was alone in the world, or did she have family out searching for her and worried sick if she was dead or alive?*

He left the questions for now and hoped she would see he meant well. Once Sara had finished eating, Brady pushed himself up from the floor and stared down at her. "I have to go now. I'll return tomorrow around this time, so you know what time to look out for me—be careful, okay?" he smiled, and she nodded.

A man of his word, Brady had shown up with food over the next five days—as promised—and sat with Sara while she ate. He wanted her to be at ease with him and wanted to share a cheerful memory about himself to make her smile. However, as he thought back into his life, his heart sank when he realised there was not much.

There was nothing since John's death that he found jovial. Everything prior had almost faded from his memory. He dug deep into his memory, searching for something therapeutic for himself. As he stared at her, a smile spread across his face when a memory came to mind.

"When I was twelve," he began, "my brother, John, and I had one of our best times at summer camp. We entered a partnered team canoe race, and we won!" He burst out laughing.

"It was such a tight race, though—with the river being rough and some of the other teams close on our tail. I remember the two teams ahead of us never seemed to carry good team spirit. All you could hear were arguments from them until, eventually, one canoe flipped over, while the other was thrown into bushes. Good thing my brother and I were always in sync with each other and coordinated well." The smile soon faded from his face as his story ended.

Sara could tell by the sudden change in his facial expression that his brother was somehow connected to his past. She timidly asked. "Where is your brother?"

"He's dead. He died a couple of months after graduating high school, just before he turned eighteen. He was so proud to join the Navy, and I was to follow him in a year," he told her, barely managing a smile. "I'm sorry. I had wanted to share something pleasant with you to make you smile and lighten your uneasiness, but I've failed," he sighed.

"But I think I can remember a time also when Gram—that's my grandmother and Mrs. Walsh, that's Gram's neighbour—used to bake the best cakes and pies. Their baking's aroma would travel all the way to the river. That was Gram's way of getting us out of the water because, as we got into our teens, we would often spend the entire day by the river," he chuckled.

"Since I returned to Gram's house, Mrs. Walsh has ordered me to come to her house for dinner each evening, so I won't be alone all the time. I think she believes that I would be feeling depressed with Gram not being there, and in some ways, she's right. She is such a sweet old lady, and you would like her. She would fatten you up before you knew it. You will love it there if you ever decide to come and stay. I hope you do," he concluded.

Sara smiled.

CHAPTER 5- RUTH'S FAREWELL GIFT

Brady closed his eyes and leant his head against the bus's window on which he rode home that evening. His mind went back to the first day he saw Sara. Remembering the dull look in her eyes, he hoped to bring light into her eyes again.

He opened his eyes, allowing the fresh evening breeze to tickle his face. A sense of accomplishment arose in him—even though small, it was something. Seeing Sara smiling while he shared stories of his past gave him hope.

As Brady disembarked the bus, he found himself smiling all the way home. He wasn't sure if it was the thought of having another person in the house or knowing that God was smiling down on him. Once inside, he ran up the stairs and headed to his grandmother's room. He needed to ensure it looked presentable to accommodate

Sara—should she decide to accept his offer. *She will come,* he thought, feeling hopeful.

Everything in the room was neatly in place, as his grandmother had always kept them. He remembered Mrs. Walsh mentioned that his grandmother had asked her to open windows now and then to let the fresh air in to avoid that old, musky smell.

"Oh, how that woman loved you, Brady," Mrs. Walsh would say.

"I love you with all my heart, Gram. I promise I won't let your hopes for me wither away," he said, glancing around the room one last time before he exited.

Before walking to his room to shower and change, he noticed his mum's old bedroom, which stood across from his grandmother's.

With his hand on the doorknob, he slowly turned it and smiled when he found it to be unlocked. The door squeaked as he pushed it open; his eyes widened, and his breath shortened at the sight.

"Oh, my! Gram!" He uttered before he fell to his knees and felt tears escaping his eyes.

Sissy boy, his father's words rang through his head as he wept. Frank would have loved to berate his emotional meltdown. It sure would have had him fuming.

Frank had a way of making his boys feel like weaklings; both John and Brady had stopped shedding tears when they entered their teens. Brady now realised that that was also around the time when he had developed his bad temper.

"How could I have allowed hate and bitterness to rob me of seeing someone's love for me?" he said as he stood and brushed off his pants. "Am I worth all this effort?"

Just then, he heard a small voice respond, *Yes, you are.* He sighed, feeling blessed, knowing that his life still had a purpose. He knew Sara's did, too.

The room was converted into a painter's studio. Walls looked recently painted his favourite colour: blue. A wooden easel stood next to the window, perhaps to use the landscape for inspiration. A large drawing table stood in the centre of the room with various paint colours in their respective jars. Alongside it was different brushes and pencils for sketching, all in varying sizes.

Brady walked a couple of paces towards the drawing table to examine its contents, then became distracted by the ajar door to his left. He ambled towards it and pushed it in. His eyes lit up, mouth agape. Over a dozen blank canvases leant against the wall, and a few aprons hung on racks. *All this for me*, he thought as he withdrew from the small room, which he presumed to have been the previous closest.

The minute he stood in front of the drawing table, an envelope stapled to the table caught his line of sight. It was addressed to him in his grandmother's handwriting. Not wanting to rip the envelope, he scanned the drawing table for a staple remover. A light shone on his face, which caused him to shield his eyes as he looked in its direction. A staple remover hung by a string from the very painting he made for his grandmother, of which she was proud.

The painting, as he remembered, reminded

him that God was omnipresent. He had been thinking hard about God's existence after a Bible lesson he and John had studied with their grandmother during a summer holiday visit. He had gone to the river and tried to capture its beauty in such a way that it would have made anyone who viewed it never doubt God.

Brady smiled at his grandmother's witty sense of humour as he took down the staple remover. He carefully removed the staples from the envelope, pulled out the letter, then walked over to the window. He sat on the stool in front of the canvas stand and began to read.

Dear Brady,

You are so special, and you don't even know it yet. I did all this for you to help you find the light that is buried within you; I know one day, it will come back to you. The Lord assures me that He has answered my prayers for you and will be there to help you. Remember, He is always near, my dearest. I know losing John was hard for you, and sometimes you still blame yourself for your mum's death. But remember that they both loved you, too, and wouldn't want you to go through life feeling defeated.

Now is your chance to live your life for all of us and show the world, especially God, that you are no longer controlled by darkness. So fight, my dear boy, to stay in the light of God, which has been waiting to wrap itself around you for so long. Look closely at the portrait you made for me when you were fourteen, and tell me if you cannot see the person I see. Don't worry, though; if you don't see him yet, just try to live your life doing good for others, and all that light will begin to shine again. I love you, Brady. Final note, 'Trust in the Lord with all your heart and lean not to your own understanding. In all your ways, acknowledge Him, and He will direct your paths.' Proverbs 3:5-6, keep your eyes on Christ. Start painting soon. Hugs and kisses from Gram.

Brady smiled as he folded the letter and placed it back into the envelope. He remembered how his grandmother always ended her letters and telephone calls with a Bible verse to strengthen him in the Lord. He took a deep breath and, this time, controlled his tears. He stood up and walked back over to the closet. He picked up one of the canvases, walked back to the window, and placed it on the canvas stand. Then he sat back down in front of it and stared blankly.

"What can I paint? Where do I even begin?" he sighed. "Lord, where do I start when all I can see in my mind are dark memories that I want to bury?"

He glanced outside as if looking for inspiration. He heard that inner voice reply. *Start with those dark memories, and meditate on my words—I remember your sins no more when you repent. Paint away all the darkness inside of you, then bury it somewhere as a symbol of letting it go. Afterwards, you can start fresh. Trust me; it will get easier. Remember, I'm always with you*

"Okay, Father, I will."

He rose and exited the room. After taking his shower, he went to the kitchen to prepare his dinner. Soon after he ate and washed the dishes, he went off to sleep.

Two days had passed since Brady discovered the studio his grandmother had left him. Her gift had brought such joy into his heart, which grew even more when he saw how at ease Sara became around him. She did not speak much but would ask one or two questions. He had not realised how lonely he was until he started visiting her.

Although he enjoyed Mrs. Walsh's company at dinnertime, the fact that he and Sara both shared a troubled past had given them a common bond. Neither had spoken of their past, but each could sense that the other had suffered something painful, heightening the comfort around each other.

As he stood to leave, as did Sara.

"Brady, I will go with you now if your offer still stands," she told him in a clear voice.

His heart swelled with such joy that he pulled her into a hug but then quickly pulled back when he realised what he did. Sara giggled, easing his anxiety.

"It still stands," he laughed as well.

As they exited the building and walked towards the bus stop. They could not wipe the smiles from their faces.

Soon, I must invest in a car, Brady thought to himself when he noticed the passerbys' looks at him and Sara. She looked so timid. He reached for her hand, hoping to ease her discomfort; she exuded no resistance when he held hers in his.

She gazed at him and saw the security he wanted to provide her. It made her smile. For the entire journey to Brady's house, she kept her gaze only on him.

CHAPTER 6- TAKING A CHANCE

They spoke no words as they walked towards the house.

While Brady inserted the key to the front door, Sara stood a few paces behind him, basking in the surroundings. *Nice and peaceful,* she thought to herself, not too isolated in case he turns out to be crazy. Finding someone to come to my rescue wouldn't be that hard.

Brady pushed open the front door then turned to glimpse Sara smiling to herself as she admired the place. "Sara, come on," he called softly.

"Nice and homely," she said to herself, stepping inside. *It does have that feminine touch,* she thought. She looked around while she followed Brady further into the house.

"Let me show you which room is yours," Brady shared as he ascended the stairs. Upon reaching the top of the stairs, he turned to face her. "You need to take a *looong* bath and get some of that stink off, Sara," he teased, pinching his nose, trying to get her to laugh at herself.

As if at impulse, Sara raised her arms, smelled her armpits, and giggled at Brady's comment. Soon, the smile fell from her face.

"Brady, . . . this is all the clothes I have, and I have no money either," she confessed.

"Come on," Brady led her to the bedroom door, "just go inside; everything you need is in there. However, if there is anything else you need, I'm in the next room," he said with a reassuring smile.

Sara nodded before she walked into the room, and then Brady left her. It was such a pleasant room; she loved it. It smelled of fresh pine. It had been a while since she had a room for herself, much less one so lovely. The walls were painted baby pink, which had always put her in a happy mood.

Sara smiled as she walked around the room, surveying everything. She glowed after spotting a writing desk stationed in front of the room's window. She could not resist the urge to run her hand across its smooth surface when she approached it.

It reminded her of those old, romantic war movies, where the woman would sit by her window. The woman would write her one true love, hoping her letters would give him the motivation and encouragement he needed to stay alive and come back to her.

Drawn to the beautiful bed lamps that stood on both sides of the bed, she dashed over to test each one. Disappointment spread across her face when she tried the first, but then her smile soon returned when she tested the other and saw its illumination.

Excitement bubbled through her. She fell backwards onto the bed, closed her eyes, and absorbed its softness. She felt such bliss that she hadn't noticed the shopping bag that lay at the foot of the bed. As she sat up, her feet knocked the bag off the bed, the sound of the contents tumbling onto the floor alerting her.

Sara jumped off the bed. Her eyes widened when she saw the feminine products that lay on the carpeted floor. She now understood why Brady told her everything she needed was inside. She knelt and began to pick up the contents one by one. Staring in amazement, her eyes welled up with tears when she realised the kind gesture Brady extended to her.

Why would he trust a stranger like me . . . when I could rob him and vanish? She thought to herself.

There were two blouses with matching skirts, a flair summer dress, underwear, deodorant, and a beautiful pair of slippers but no bra.

"He has such great taste," she said aloud, smiling. "But . . . how did he even know what would fit me?" she arched her brow, pondering.

Happiness filled her as she chose what she would put on and then went into the bathroom and locked the door behind her. Her smile broadened even more when she saw fresh towels on racks, a toothbrush, and toothpaste on the face basin.

Sara glanced at her reflection in the mirror, and her smile faded. She stared hard, hoping to find some trace of the beautiful, happy girl she once was. Her eyes had such dark circles and her skin looked blotchy. Even her once beautiful, tamed dark waves now were frizzy and unkempt.

She opened the mirrored cabinet door, and her smile returned when she saw bath soap, shampoo, conditioner, and even a first-aid kit.

"He really went all out for me."

After turning on the tap, she left it to fill up while she stripped off the filthy remains of her clothes, which she had decided to later burn. However, realising she needed her bra, she pulled it from the heap and washed it. Then she placed it on a rack to dry, just before she stepped into the bath and soaked her battered body into the soothing warm water.

"Thank you, Jesus," she said while scrubbing the dirt from her skin. As she washed her hair, she had heard a knock on her door. Brady's voice mumbled through the door. Panic filled her before she realised that she had locked the bathroom door. "Don't come in! I'm still in the shower!" she shouted.

"Don't panic, Sara!" Brady said in a loud voice to ensure she heard him. "I just came to tell you I'm going downstairs to prepare dinner. Come down when you're ready, okay?"

The sound of his footsteps clobbering down the stairs brought her a sigh of relief. By the time she had finished showering, she had stepped out of the shower and took a second look at her reflection in the mirror. This time, she smiled; the reflection did not look as beat as before. *Still*, the beauty she once had seemed somewhat lost.

The smell of food reminded her of Brady. Sara hurried and dressed. She dried most of her hair before she joined him. She entered the kitchen and saw Brady washing his hands. She strolled over to the kitchen table. "Brady."

Brady turned to face her.

"Thank you for the clothes and everything else you have done for me. You didn't have to do any of that, yet you did. For that, I am very grateful."

Brady smiled, and his face lit up as he stared at Sara. She had lovely caramel skin and beautiful eyes, which gleamed some measure of happiness. Her hair, pinned up in a tidy bun, looked so soft and healthy. And her smile forced him to take notice of her beautiful, full lips. Although she stood at only five feet one, she looked very much a woman.

"You look so pretty, Sara. Now I finally get to see the woman beneath the dirt," he teased, causing her to blush. "And it was my pleasure."

"Brady, how did you know my size?" she asked, looking a little confused.

"Well, I took a mental picture of your physique when I brought you food. Later, I went to a store and looked for a shop assistant that had a similar body type as yours, and she helped me pick out those clothes for you. I'm sorry I didn't get you a bra, though," he chuckled. "I wasn't sure about how to ask her about that, seeing you and her have different sizes. We can go back tomorrow to get you more clothes, and you can pick out what you need. And don't worry about it," he stressed. "I don't mind." He spun around to the oven when he heard the timer go off and opened it. "Dinner is ready. Can you help me set the table?"

"Sure."

Sara scampered over to the oven and stood next to him.

"Do you like baked chicken and potatoes?" Brady smiled at her when he removed the potatoes from the oven. "It's one of the few dishes my mum taught me."

A coy smile curled on Sara's lips. "I do." She took the dish of potatoes from his hand and strolled to the dinner table while Brady took the chicken out of the oven and followed her.

As soon as they placed the chicken and potatoes on the table, they returned to the cooking area and collected plates, utensils, and juice from the fridge.

Sitting down to a nice meal in such a quiet and peaceful environment was a new experience for Sara. Both she and Brady had come to appreciate the blessing of a home-cooked meal. They sat, staring at each other for a while, unsure of what to say.

"My Gram used to make us hold hands and pray before we ate our meals. I think that's the right thing to do," Brady said a few minutes later to break the awkward silence.

He reached over to take her hands. Sara's heart beat a little faster when she placed her hands in his. Although somewhat nervous by his touch, she felt safe.

"My family used to do it, also," she added.

"Father, for what we are about to eat, we

give you thanks for providing. We ask you to bless it. Protect us with your righteous right hand and the blood of Jesus, who gave His life for us. We ask You to guide us each day and help us throughout this journey we call life. Keep us on the path You have set before us. In Jesus's name, we pray. Amen."

"Amen," Sara added.

They ate dinner without words. Even while doing the dishes, they kept quiet but laughed at each other when the tap accidentally sprayed them when Brady turned it on.

"It's been quite a long day, Sara; I'm off to bed now. I'll see you in the morning," Brady told her as soon as they had put the last dish away.

He trudged up the stairs, walked into his room, then strolled over to the window and closed it. He had left it open all evening to let some of the chill night air enter his room to keep it nice and cool while he slept. He walked over to his bed, plopped down, and kicked off his boots. Stretching out, he closed his eyes when his head hit his soft pillows. However, he kept seeing the blank canvas.

Brady opened his eyes and exhaled aloud. After reading his grandmother's letter, he had planned to start painting the next day, but fear came over him. Bringing all that pain back to the surface was not what he was ready for, so he had put it off until the day after.

He had woken up that morning with some courage and strength to begin painting. Even having gone into the studio, he laid aside all the brushes and paint he would need to work with. However, he wanted to wait until after he returned home from his visit with Sarah. Seeing her made him feel happy.

That was something he knew would help him break through those dark memories—only he didn't expect her to accept his offer today, so he was beat after dinner. *Tomorrow*, he thought to himself, rolling over onto his side and closed his eyes again.

A negative voice crept into his head. *Are you sure you can trust that woman in your house? How can you trust someone you found on the streets looking the way she did? How do you know she didn't murder someone and is just on the run?*

Brady sat up in bed and stared in the direction of his window. The sky looked bright, stars glimmered. He pondered on all the thoughts swirling around in his head. Then he tried to place himself in her shoes. He wondered if people thought the same of him when he lived on the streets.

"No!" he said aloud. "I won't listen to you, Satan. Everyone deserves a second chance, even I did. God, I will leave it all in your hands and trust that You are with me and will guide me in doing right by Sara. She might be a blessing more to me than I will be to her."

Brady sighed and then fell back onto his pillow. This time, he drifted off to sleep.

Sara switched the kitchen light off and ambled her way towards the front door. She tipped on her toes and stared outside through the small, glass-framed window built into the door. It all looked so perfect. Everything seemed so at peace: the trees, the stars in the sky, the few houses along the pathway, even the sounds of wild animals in the woods. She wondered if this could become home for her and Brady—like a family, something she had long hoped to have again.

"Lord, reveal to me your plans for my life," she prayed.

Sara tried to suppress the tears that fought to stream down her face. She turned her gaze from the door and stared up the stairs. She wondered how a man who seemed to have his own demons could be so kind-hearted, unassuming, and trusting her alone in his house.

Maybe helping me is his way of overcoming his past, she thought, and with that, she climbed the stairs and went to bed.

CHAPTER 7- A FRESH START

Living on the streets had forced Sara to become cautious of her surroundings and an early riser. Her eyes fluttered open, and she smiled, getting her first glimpse of the sun rising as the light penetrated the room. She dashed out of bed and ran to the window to get a better view.

A brilliant shade of golden light spread across the blue canvas. It made her think of God smiling and saying: *embrace the beauty of a new day given to you and forget the darkness of yesterday. This is your time to step out of the shadows and embrace the beginning of new life and the hope given.* She felt God's love.

As the sun took its place in the heavens, Sara inhaled the fresh morning air. The river below brought her thoughts to the stories Brady shared of times he and John spent there. It was indeed a beautiful sight.

It made her miss going to the beach with her best friend, Jessica. A feeling of guilt came over her as she thought back to how she had turned her back on Jessica when Jessica tried to help her get through a difficult time in her life. Except what Jessica didn't know is that it was all too inconceivable; the shame of it made it even harder to talk about.

Sara cleared her mind of such thoughts and sauntered into the bathroom to freshen up. She thought it would be a nice gesture to prepare breakfast, so she tiptoed down the stairs as not to wake Brady. Inside the kitchen, she searched through the refrigerator and cupboards to see what kind of food Brady had in the house.

Eggs, milk, cheese, sweet peppers, and sausage, all the ingredients to prepare omelettes. A memory flashed before her: her mum standing behind her, holding her hand as she whisks eggs in a bowl. Her mother was of mixed heritage—Venezuelan and Jamaican and had taught her a lot in both cooking styles. Her mother had also taught her to speak Spanish and the Jamaican dialect because she believed in preserving the cultures.

Sara smiled, feeling a bit like her old self, and hummed a tune as she turned the eggs. While the eggs cooked, she paused, wondering whether Brady preferred coffee to tea.

"I'll take a chance with tea; I think he'll enjoy that."

She removed the omelettes from the frying pan, placed them onto two plates, and carried them over to the table. As she turned to walk back to the kitchen counter, Brady walked in, and she flinched by his sudden presence.

"You scared me, Brady," she giggled and pressed her hand to her chest, taking in a deep breath.

Brady chuckled, "Sorry, didn't mean to; I was never one to make loud entrances." He pulled out a chair at the table and sat down.

Sara continued towards the kitchen counter and reached for a tray and two mugs.

"Want any help?" Brady pushed back his chair and stood.

"No! Sit back down; I can handle it," she smiled.

Brady leaned back against the chair and inhaled deeply. "*Hmmm*, something smells really good. I didn't know you cooked, Sara."

Sara blushed and whispered. "My mom taught me when she was alive." She then added the teapot to the tray.

"She died?" his brow arched in surprise.

"Yes, of leukaemia—when I was sixteen."

"Death seems to be all around us. Lurking in the shadows—like the devil, who goes around roaring, seeking whom he may devourer."

Sara lifted the tray and walked back to the table. She poured some tea into the two mugs before she settled in her seat. "I had to start cooking for Dad and myself after Mum died, seeing he didn't know how to. That's when I grew to become very good at it," she shared, much to her surprise at how easy it was for her to open up to Brady.

A smile spread across Brady's face while he stared at her.

"Why do you stare at me and smile?" she

asked.

"It's just good to have you here, Sara. You know what? Let's go out on the deck and eat; you'll see the best view of the river from there, and the breeze is always refreshing."

"Sounds like a marvellous idea," she agreed.

They took their breakfast and walked out to the deck.

Truly, this is the best view of the river from the house, Sara thought as she sat down. *Whoever built this deck aimed to take in the majesty of this nature's wonder, making it a wonderful asset to the landscape.*

"Brady, it's so beautiful out here. Look at all those birds; they are so beautiful! I bet they attract bird lovers from all over." Her smile grew even more.

"They sure do, ever since I was a child, visiting Gram, John and I would always see many people come around here. The Green Ash and Red Maple trees you see there are what attract the birds. The visitors—although they came for the birds—could never miss the opportunity to relax in Wolf River's cooling waters," he chuckled.

"There are a lot of flowers down there, too, it seems," she continued, staring out towards the river.

"This area is very lush, and when you get closer, you will see lots more and how beautiful they are. Now eat before the food gets cold," he teased.

Sara felt safe, and all the horrors she was running from seemed to disappear at that moment. She glanced over at the man who sat alongside her and smiled as she watched him chewing on his omelette, while staring at the river.

"You are happy, aren't you?" he asked her, without removing his eyes from the river.

Could he sense I was smiling? she thought to herself. "Yes, Brady, I am. Thank you."

"Stop thanking me, Sara. You would have done the same for me, too, if you were in my shoes," he told her, turning now to face her.

"Would I?" she responded, wondering if she had it in her to do the same.

"Yes, you would. I can sense it in you. You have a lot of good inside of you, even if you don't believe it anymore," he replied with much faith.

"But how can you know that about me after knowing me for such a short time?"

"Something in me keeps telling me to trust you, and I feel a sense of comfort around you," he smiled. "It's strange how after leaving that horrible place—Lexington— the first person I met is you. If I had not placed my life into God's hands, I probably would have seen you and not cared. The thing is, I feel so at ease talking with you, and you don't judge me. And for me to move on from who I was and where I'd been, I needed that, so thank you, too."

The sky looked beautiful with a few clouds in the sky, the trees swayed in the soft wind that blew, and the coolness of the day relaxed Sara and Brady.

After they had finished breakfast, Brady turned to Sara once more and asked, "Would you like to go into town with me now to buy you some more personal items and maybe help me do some grocery shopping?"

"Yes," she smiled and nodded.

Within a few minutes, Sara washed the dishes, then she and Brady left for town. This time, the bus ride was not so unpleasant for her as when she left with Brady. She no longer looked filthy or felt so uneasy by the passengers' glares.

Although she still had her guard up around Brady, he was the first sign of hope she had found. She wanted to see if by giving him the chance to prove his true intentions; it meant God had finally looked down on her, wrapping His arms around her, and delivering her from all the hurt the world had inflicted on her.

With Brady next to her, Sara felt bolder, stepping out again amongst people. They strolled through the clothing store, picking out different items for her to try. Brady laughed at some of her fashion choices before offering to help her.

"Sara, why don't you try these?" he said, stretching two outfits in her direction.

She laughed, taking the outfits from Brady before trying them on. His laugh was so contagious; she loved his smile and how helpful he was. Sara found herself being playful, laughing at how shy he became when she asked his opinion on different bras.

Although the experience was new to them both, they found it comforting. It helped them get better acquainted with each other. Getting groceries made them very cheerful.

"Brady, will you allow me to prepare meals for us while I stay at your house? It's the least I can do after all you have done for me," Sara asked as they pushed the shopping cart through the meat aisle.

"I would love that, Sara; that would be great," he chuckled. "I'll just give you a list of the things I need, and you can just add them to what you want to buy for the house."

Sara smiled. Soon, she and Brady walked out of the grocery store with two bags full of groceries and took the first bus back to the house. Seemed they both like the isolation from the prying eyes of people they thought were always judging them.

Once back at the house, they walked into the kitchen and unpacked the grocery bags to put the food items away.

"Brady, I can do that," Sara said when he walked to the fridge with the milk carton.

"Are you sure?"

She nodded and smiled.

"Alright," he turned towards the door, "I'll be upstairs if you need anything."

"Okay."

Brady climbed the stairs two-by-two, walked to his studio door, and paused. He closed his eyes and took a deep breath. *Start with the dark memories,* came the words of the Holy Spirit again.

Brady pushed open the door and traversed into the studio. He stepped over to the easel stand and stared down at it. A few seconds passed. His eyes instinctively turned to the river outside the window as if to awaken his inspiration from it.

An image of the last time he saw his brother, John, alive came to mind, and a tear fell.

"I don't know if I can do this," he spoke, barely audible.

Be strong in the Lord and the power of his might. A Bible verse his grandmother, Ruth, often shared with him to encourage him when fear tried to set in came to mind.

Brady wiped the tear stream from his cheeks and treaded slowly over to the table with the paint supplies and brushes. He reached for the white and black, along with two brushes and his palette, before he walked back to the easel and sat down.

Dipping his brush into the mixture of paint, he soon was engrossed in bringing to life the image in his mind.

CHAPTER 8- DISCOVERING LIFE AGAIN

Left to herself downstairs, Sara finished putting away the groceries and sighed. She reached for the shopping bag on top of the kitchen counter with her new clothing and personal items. She smiled, eager to pick out one of the outfits to wear later after her evening bath.

She walked towards the staircase, but her attention was averted to the living room next to it. Sara stepped inside as the sight of the memory-filled room enchanted her. *Brady's grandmother sure knew how to preserve family moments*, she thought.

Staring at all the photos, she did not have to guess too hard to tell who was who. Each one was arranged in the order in which they were taken. It was such an inviting family room; it reminded her of her home when everything was good and everyone happy.

Sara's eyes soon caught sight of the very thing she loved more than anything—a piano. It was a beautiful white grand and still looked brand new. Before she knew it, she sat in front of it and had her fingers running over the keys with a big grin on her face.

She played each key, familiarising herself with their sounds until she was lost in a beloved melody—which for years, she thought was lost. Now, sitting once again in front of a piano, made it come right back.

From upstairs, Brady heard the piano playing and smiled, knowing Sara was making herself at home. He was unsure of what she liked since she had not really opened up about herself yet. Hearing her play made him content, knowing that she found comfort in at least something in his house. She played well, and he presumed that she must have had many years of training.

Sara sat, playing for nearly an hour, then felt she wanted to test the river waters that Brady bragged about so much. She ran upstairs into her room, picked out a pair of shorts and a blouse to swim in. She laid the dress she wanted to wear later on the bed and put everything else away in the dresser. She didn't feel comfortable wearing a swimsuit around a man she was still getting to know. Sara walked out of her room, strolled over to Brady's room, and knocked on the door.

"Brady," she called.

Getting no response, she tried the knob and found it unlocked. She pushed the door and glanced inside, then closed it when she didn't see him. A door that stood ajar on the opposite side to both her room and Brady's piqued her curiosity.

Sara walked across the hallway to the door and peeped inside. Brady sat, painting. He looked so consumed in what he was painting, which looked very foreboding. There was not one ounce of colour on the canvas. Her heart softened to what must be buried inside him. She wondered how he managed to maintain a sense of calmness around her yet hold such darkness inside.

Could his past be even worse than mine?

Sara sneaked away and made her way outside the house, down the dirt tracks towards the river.

"Wow!"

It was beautiful, and Sara saw all the way to the bottom. She even recognised a few of the flowers from the deck: the blue phloxes, spatterdocks, and the ironweed.

"*Ahhh.*" She exhaled, dipping her toes into the cool water.

As much as she wanted to quietly enjoy the river and not alert Brady, she could not resist the urge and jumped into the water. She made such a splash and sank to the bottom. After emerging again, she floated around on the surface.

Even if the source came from just enjoying one of nature's wonders, she was happy. She could easily find inspiration in this surroundings and could already hear new melodies floating around in her head. At that moment, she giggled, feeling free from the memories of her past. In her contentment, she had even forgotten about

Brady.

She must have spent about an hour by the river before she got out and made her way back up to the house. Sara went straight to her room, showered, then came down and started dinner. Even when she finished preparing dinner and set the table, Brady still had not left the studio. Sara was almost afraid to disturb him after seeing his dark painting.

"Brady!" she shouted from the foot of the stairs, "Dinner's ready!"

She walked back into the kitchen, took a seat at the dinner table, and waited. Within a few minutes, he came strolling into the kitchen with a smile, which made her nervous.

"Brady, are you alright?" she asked, concern etched across her face.

"Yes, I'm okay. Why do you ask that?"

"I'm afraid to say."

"Come on, tell me. I'm not going to bite," he took a seat at the table facing her.

"Well, earlier today, after I went to my room to place the clothes you bought me inside, I saw the door to your studio ajar. I peeped in and saw you consumed in a painting that looked so dark. It kind of . . . scared me. Makes me wonder if you are like some kind of Doctor Jekyll and Mr. Hyde," she confessed.

Brady laughed at her comparison of him to a crazy book character. "Well, for your information, it's my way of relieving myself of the dark past I had. The Lord advised me to paint away the darkness, and the light will come. My grandmother always saw the light in me, too, and always prayed for me that it will come. It was her who did all that for me—the studio and all you see in there, I mean. When I'm ready, I will tell you everything about my past or just let you see it from the paintings, okay?" he assured her.

"Come on, let's eat. No more worries, okay? There is no monster in me waiting to jump out and attack you, just like there is no monster in you that will jump out and scare me either. Though painful as our past may be, they sometimes help us see the world from a different perspective. If we did not experience what we did, maybe others who have been or still are in situations as we were would not be of any interest to us even to reach out to help. God is always near us, even in the worst times, Sara."

"You're right, Brady. Sorry for comparing you to a crazy monster," she chuckled. "I hope you like dinner."

"It looks yummy, too. Mmmm," he said as he tasted it.

"Hey, . . . we haven't prayed yet," she reminded him.

"Oh, yes, forgive me. I just could not wait to taste it. Let's pray," he said.

While they were enjoying dinner, Brady blurted out, "I see you've found the piano, and you play it so well, too. Where did you learn?"

Sara smiled shyly. "I started learning when I was five; my dad used to teach me at home."

"That's great. My Gram tried to teach John and me, but only John took a liking to it. He played well, too. I can play the guitar, though. I think mine's still there in the living room somewhere. Gram kept everything. I was more interested in painting. I only learned to play the guitar to play alongside John and to also make Gram happy. Sara, I hope you don't mind me asking you about yourself. You don't have to tell me anything if you're not ready to answer now, okay?" he told her before throwing in another question. "So, where is your dad? Is he also deceased?"

"No, Brady, he is not dead. But I'm not ready to talk about him just yet."

"It's alright, let's just finish this delicious meal. You truly are a good cook," he complimented her as they dug into the meal.

For the next two weeks, their routines were monotonous. Brady kept himself locked up in his studio after they had breakfast, leaving Sara to herself. She found that while she sat at the piano, many songs floated in her head. She began to write musical sheets, and soon after, she would practice playing them.

Although Brady was consumed in his own world, he thoroughly enjoyed listening to her play. Her music seemed reflective of a heavenly place in which they both yearn to be. However, she would sometimes play something dark, which made him cringe, wondering if she had seen inside his soul and had created something that reflected just that. Then he would realise they must have been a reflection of her own dark past.

After spending time at the piano creating music, Sara would slip away to the river to enjoy the solitude, which seemed to inspire her music. She had no idea that Brady had noticed she sneaked off to the river. She was afraid to have him go with her. Sometimes he would stand at his window and watch her float around on the water and just smile.

It did not matter to him what brought her contentment at that moment. It pleased him, knowing she was not hurting so much anymore, and he waited patiently for her to be ready to open up to him. He longed to talk about his own demons, but would she be able to handle *his*? Even *he* hated the person whom he became; why should she not hate him as well?

CHAPTER 9- DIGGING UP OLD WOUNDS

"Brady, do you know that since I came to your house just over two weeks ago, you have been crying out almost every other night in your sleep, and it's always about your mum?" Sara said with her eyes on Brady as they sat on the deck having breakfast.

"I have?" he arched a brow in surprise.

"Yes, and it's always the same words. 'Mum, I'm sorry. I love you.' I know it's tormenting you, and I worry about you because of it," she sympathised. "Each night I hear you, I pray to God to show me how to help you get past it. And right after I pray, I end up feeling like I have no right to ask such a thing."

"Why?"

"Because you took me in and hid nothing in your house from me, knowing you were taking a big risk. It's like I keep thinking, how can I expect you to share your troubles with me when I still struggle with trusting your sincerity after all you have done for me?"

"It's all right, Sara. I understand that it sometimes takes a while to truly see the good in someone, especially if you have been through something that causes you to doubt everyone and everything."

"I'm sorry, Brady. I do trust you, it's . . . it's just habit, and it's taking a while to let go of it."

Brady turned to face Sara with a gleam of sadness in his eyes. "Sara, I broke my mother's heart, and now she's dead. I can't tell her how much I loved her and appreciated her." He fought back the tears that threatened to fall.

"Brady, I'm sure your mum loved you no matter what and would have forgiven you if she were here. Let it go and just accept that she loved you. She wouldn't want to see you beating yourself up as you do—would she?"

"No, she wouldn't, and she would have forgiven me, too. That's why it's so hard to let go sometimes. To know that even after whatever I did, she always had a calm demeanour. She never raised her voice at me and always waited to just hold me in her arms. Sometimes the way she would hug me made me think she probably thought it might be her last."

"After my mum died," Sara quietly began, causing Brady to give her his undivided attention. "It became hard for both Dad and me. He's a police officer, and while at work, his mind was usually kept busy and away from missing Mum. For me, though, the moment I wake up, I would miss her. No more knocks on my door waking me up to get ready for school, no more of the aroma of freshly prepared breakfast. I had to prepare food for Dad and me.

"Dad usually dropped me off at school, so it was okay at school. But when I'd walk to the gate after school, waiting to see Mum there with her glowing smile, tears would stream down my face. It reminded me that she's gone. My friend, Jessica, was always so supportive and comforted me on our way home each day.

"Dad, on the other hand, tried to hide his feelings for my sake. For a while, it was okay even at dinner with just the two of us. I managed to finish my final year in high school and did very well on my final exams. I wanted to make my parents proud, and since it was just Dad and me, I wanted to ease the burden off of him. I knew he was still hurting, even though he hid it from me. He was so proud of me. I can still remember the look on his face when he saw me graduate." By saying this, she broke down.

Brady stretched his hand across the table and took hers. "Hey, . . . you don't have to talk about it now," he said with a gentle voice.

"I want to, Brady. If I don't, I won't ever get past this, and I really need to. *Will you listen?* This is the first time I'm talking to anyone about it. I just never felt comfortable telling anyone about any of it until now. I felt too ashamed and didn't want to see anyone's eyes shifting from pity to shame. But I don't feel that with you, and I have wanted to tell someone for so long. So *please* will you listen?" she sobbed.

Brady got up from his chair and stood in front of Sara. "Yes, I'll listen as long as you want me to. Come here." He opened his arms, inviting her into a hug.

Sara stared up at him for a moment before she eased up out of her chair and walked into his embrace.

As Sara wept in Brady's arms, the memories of seeing his mum shedding tears flashed before him, and it tore at his heart. He took a deep breath and squeezed his eyes shut, blocking out the past from interfering with comforting Sara. *She needed him, and he needed to be there for her.*

"Come. Let's sit over there." He led her over to the much wider chair on the deck. He then used his broad fingers to wipe the tears from her eyes and urged her to continue.

Sara took a deep breath. "It wasn't until the following year that things started to get crazy. I was now back to myself again; although I missed Mum a lot, I was now coping better. I had wanted to go to college to study music. However, Dad was not doing too well, so I decided to postpone for a year, hoping he would finally accept that Mum was not coming back.

"I got a job working in a bank close to home, which gave me time to get home and still make dinner for Dad. I could hear him weeping in his room night after night, and I tried my best not to follow suit. I wanted to be strong for both of us. He started smoking to try to deal with it. Everyone thought he was doing okay; no one around him saw the signs. His loud sobs woke me up one night; that night, it seemed, he had reached his breaking point."

CHAPTER 10- A VERY DARK PERIOD

"The room was dark, and I got worried; my parents never slept in total darkness. Most nights, they kept one of their bedside lamps on. I almost tripped over Dad's feet when I walked over to where he sat on the bed after discovering that the switch by the door did not work. Dad just sat there . . . in total darkness. I did not know how to make his pain go away. All that came to my mind as I faced him was to hug him.

"But, as I hugged him, it made him sob harder. Then when he hugged me back, he squeezed so tight that I had to beg him to let go. I heard his muffled voice saying, '*Monica, I have missed you.*' I tried to tell him that it was me and not Mum, but it seemed my voice convinced him I was Mum. His hands began to caress my body, and I froze, thinking he would snap out of it— only he didn't. He threw me on the bed and climbed on top of me.

"Fear consumed me at this point. I began to wonder what was going through his mind as he stared down into my face. I thought he was going to kill me—then himself. He had not smiled much since Mum died. I pleaded with him to come back to being the dad that I missed and needed. Instead, he kept on muttering, *'I missed you, sweetheart.'*

"I thought my dad had gone crazy. He raised his hand to my face, and I closed my eyes, fearing the worst. He began to caress my cheeks the way I used to see him caress Mum's. I started to cry, telling him that it was me—*Sara*, not Mum. Before I could say anything else, I felt his lips pressing hard against mine.

"All the while, I fought to resist him, but he kept saying, *'Monica, I missed you so much.'* I cried harder. My dad had truly gone insane. Soon, he began to remove my pyjamas, and I screamed in terror—I screamed even harder when I felt his nakedness. He kissed me hard to suppress the screams while he forced himself into me and stole my virginity." Sara fell against Brady's chest as she wept again.

Brady could not believe what he was hearing. *How could such things happen?* He fought hard to suppress the rage surfacing at hearing what Sara just revealed to him. He cradled her head against his chest and gently consoled her.

"Sara, are you sure you want to talk about this now? I'm not going anywhere, so we can continue another time," he suggested, thinking she might need a break from letting out all these memories at once.

Sara pulled away from his embrace and shook her head. "No, I have to finish this today, Brady," she pleaded.

"Alright, just take your time," he whispered.

"Brady, I felt so confused with the whole incident. After my dad finished raping me, he fell over and slept. I ran to the bathroom and sat in a tub of water in a daze. Not even tears came while I sat there. I did not know whether to hate him or feel sorry for him. After all, I loved my dad, but who I left in my parent's bedroom, I did not know.

"I think I must have sat there the whole night. When I was tired and started slipping below the water's surface instead of getting out, I just sat back up and continued staring absent-mindedly. My dad found me in the morning, shivering when he came to use the bathroom. He was completely lost to what had happened the night before," she lamented.

"Like a concerned father, he rushed in, grabbed a towel, and wrapped me in it. Then he took me to my bedroom, lay me in bed, and sat by my bedside, weeping at the state of my condition. After a few minutes, he grabbed the phone and tried to call for an ambulance, when I pulled his arm."

Sara continued. "Though in my shocked state, I informed him of what happened the night before. He staggered back against the wall and slid onto the floor, weeping and alarmed by what he had done. I found myself sympathetic towards him and told him I forgave him—that he was not himself. But he wouldn't accept that he could do such a terrible thing, much less to his own flesh and blood.

"He called in sick that day to take care of me and did a good job, too. He called my workplace and told them I was not feeling well. It took me three days to get back on my feet and get back to work. For the next three weeks, my dad seemed okay; he even quit smoking and started smiling again.

"I remember how, at dinner, he often told me that I was looking more like Mum. Once upon a time, I would have been happy to hear that, but after what had transpired between us, hearing that made me nervous. Since then, I started sleeping with my door locked. Next time it happened—"

"It happened again?" Brady interrupted, wide-eyed. Sara darted a glare at him. He could see that she was not pleased that he interrupted her. "Sorry, continue," he apologised.

"The next time it happened," Sara started again, "Dad came home drunk. His friends from the force had taken him out to drink. Dad was never much of a drinker, so he got drunk fast. I had just finished preparing dinner, felt hot and sticky, and had gone to shower. I did not hear him sneak into the bathroom and panicked when I saw his shadow appear against the shower curtain.

"I tried to jump out when I saw him hop in. Dad had always been strong, even while drunk. He had always been physically fit and strong. He grabbed my arm just as I stepped out of the tub. I pleaded with him, but he kept smiling and being playful, thinking I was Mum again.

'Monica, you are so beautiful when you're playing hard to get,' he said to me. Then he threw me over his shoulder, took me to his bedroom, and raped me again.

"This time, I didn't bother moving. I just laid there as the tears streamed down my face. By morning, he woke up to find me lying next to him. He did not bother to ask me what happened—he knew. When he tried to touch me, trying to be apologetic, I pulled away. Still naked, I got up and walked out, hoping that in his now-sober state, seeing his daughter naked would break him free of whatever had possessed him to do such a thing.

"I locked myself in my room and didn't answer when he banged on the door, begging and pleading with me to forgive me. He said he did not know what possessed him. Even when my closest friend, Jessica, called—because I did not show up for work two days in a row without calling or sending a note—I just let her think I had a nervous breakdown because of Mum's death. I made her believe that I had not gotten over it the entire time.

"I hated what Dad did to me, but I couldn't bear the shame if everyone found out what he did. I didn't want the world to see my dad as a monster. I still loved him. He was all I had. Before Mum died, he was the best father in the world. He taught me how to play the piano and how to ride a bicycle. He and Mum were always a team. Mum didn't have to call Dad to remind him about my school track events or my piano recitals just to be supportive. Whenever Mum was busy with something, he would always be there for me.

"How could I forget all that because of what I now suffered? I was torn, trying to hold to who my dad was and letting go of who he had become. I was scared every day. Every day, I got up, made his breakfast and lunch, then went back to my room. I had lost my job by then and did not care. I could not face anyone, nor did I want to. I did not want to deal with questions about my "nervous breakdown." Eventually, I would have ended up spilling about Dad, and it would have been too devastating.

"I would later come out, make his dinner, leave it on the table, and then go back to my room and lock the door. Every night, he'd be at my door with sincere concern in his voice, wanting to know how I was, profusely apologising. It was not until he threatened to kill himself and hearing him cock his gun that I came out of the room, allowing him to hug me.

"Six weeks had passed since then, and we were casual again, like roommates. He didn't bother me much. He just wanted to see things come back to normal and allowed me to come around at my own pace. Then, almost every morning since those six weeks passed, I got sick in the mornings, and I developed a really bad fever with it, which caused Dad to grow concerned. He took me to see a doctor. We both were shocked when the doctor told us that I was pregnant . . ."

"Pregnant?"

"Yes, Brady, pregnant. Dad panicked, thinking his life was now over. When the doctor asked about the father, I told him the father ran out on me when he found out I was pregnant. My dad stared at me, shocked by my response. He wept, causing the poor doctor to pat his back and console him. The doctor told him that I would be fine, especially having a concerned father like him—how ironic, right?" she chuckled sarcastically.

"When we got back home, we sat in the living room, wondering what to do next. It might sound strange to you after hearing all that, but my parents were devoted Christians, and I loved growing up knowing the Lord and his ways. It was probably why I could not find myself hating my father and even found myself forgiving him. Although all he did to me was sinful, I could not add more to it now by having an abortion. I told him I would not do it, and I just left it to God for what to do next.

"My father, instead of continuing being the spiritual head of our family as he was before Mum died, had allowed the devil to play upon his sorrow. The devil sent a demon to him, which plagued him and caused him to molest me when he did. I had tried to pray to God, despite everything, and not grow bitter against Him or my father. But when it happened a third time, I gave up on both."

CHAPTER 11- TREADING UNKNOWN WATERS

"Dad came home drunk and angry again a month after we found out I was pregnant. I had made his dinner and left it on the table, took my bath, and rested in my room. His loud and heavy footsteps woke me up, but I did not go out to find out what was wrong.

"It was safer to stay where I was. I just did not think that he would do what he did twice to me, now while I was pregnant, so I did not rush to close my door, and I was very exhausted. Dad barged into my room, and this time, I couldn't see my dad in that face. He looked so angry that I did not even bother to scream . . . for fear he might hurt me.

"He left the room when he was done and went to his room and slept. He snored so loud that I could hear it from my room. By morning, I went to the bathroom to pee and saw a pool of blood in the toilet. I knew I lost the baby due to the amount of blood. Even when it stopped, and I managed to go see the doctor, the bleeding started again. The doctor confirmed that I had, indeed, lost it.

"I was somewhat sad and relieved at the same time. All the while, I was wondering what I would do with a child whose father is my own father. What would I have told it? Could I even bear to keep it?"

"Where was your dad when you went to the doctor alone?"

"He was still sleeping. When I returned home and packed my bags, he was still asleep. That was the last time I saw my dad, but I had left him a letter before I left. Do you want to know what I wrote?"

Brady shook his head, eager to know.

"Well, I think this is what I wrote":

Dear Dad,

By the time you get this, I will be gone. You have hurt me so much when you were supposed to protect me. Mum died, and you were supposed to be there for me as I tried to be for you. Instead, you allowed the devil to use you to inflict so much harm on me and even robbed me of the very thing I wanted to save for my marriage. You were the one who used to tell me to save it for that special person that God has kept just for you, and you robbed me of that. Will that special guy still want me after I tell him about my past, excluding the fact that it was my dad? Even though you hurt me, Dad, I could never let the world think of you as a monster.

Please repent and find your way back to

Christ. Pray for him to deliver you from whatever demon that possessed you each time you saw me as Mum. I need to be away from you at this point in my life if I want to keep my sanity and not end up hating you. For the father who you once were to me, I choose to leave and remember you that way. I hope that when the Lord says I should come back home, by then, you will be my old Dad again. I love you still, Dad; I just hate what you did to me. I just can't be around you now. And if you ever think of killing yourself, know that you will have caused my death in doing so. So, please stay alive and fight the demon you have called upon yourself and pray for the Lord to restore our family. Please do not look for me. I will call you every once in a while so you know I am okay and make sure that you are. Your daughter,
Sara.

"I switched off my phone after telling my friend, Jessica, that I was going away for a while. However, she pleaded with me to stay with her, and for a week, I did, just to make her feel better. However, knowing the terrible secret I kept and afraid that I would spill it out somehow, I left when she went out for some groceries.

"I only took one of my bags this time and hopped on the first bus out of town. I got off at its final destination. I do not even remember what that town was called. I have been to so many since then, I cannot count. I rented a room at a motel and managed to get a nice job in a small office with my banking experience. I was even doing okay for the first six months at that job. Then the boss started making passes at me, and when I refused him, he fired me.

"I got another job in that same town, and this time, someone broke into my room and stole most of my stuff. When I reported it to the police, they were not much help. They said they had no suspects and were working to see what could be done. Over the next few months, nothing came out of that, and so I never retrieved those things.

"By the time I turned twenty, working at the next office, I had managed to save up some money to purchase back some of the things that were stolen. I went out and had a quiet dinner to celebrate my birthday. Later, I called my father just to hear a familiar voice, but I didn't speak. He knew it was me, though. He talked; I just listened.

"He sounded so worried and scared for me. I wanted so much to run to my daddy for comfort, but that dad was not there anymore. You know, it seemed that since my dad raped me, a spirit like what came over him followed me everywhere. The boss at the second office tried the same thing as the first one, and when I refused him, he, too, fired me. I left and went to another town; the same thing happened.

"By this time, I was so stressed, I ended up in the shelters. I was too scared to be around men. I thought the isolation would help me deal with my struggles. I hadn't even prayed since my last encounter with my dad to even find out what to do. I just thought God hated me by allowing all these to transpire in my life when I had been faithful while growing up.

"Somehow, the shelter proved to be worse, instead of helping. I found that they brought their handful of dangers, especially to a single twenty-year-old young woman. I had to sleep with an eye open; perverts and thieves were everywhere. I only stayed at a handful of shelters and always for short periods. The last shelter I stayed at, I was raped and beaten by two men. That was two years ago."

"Oh, my God!" Brady blurted out, shocked.

"You alright, Brady?" Sara asked, concerned by the frightened look on his face.

"Yeah, I am. I am just so surprised you went through all that."

"Well, next thing I knew, I woke up in a hospital so traumatised that they decided to keep me in there for a month, for fear that I would end my life. I had thought of it, too, Brady, quite a few times. It was there in the hospital that I prayed to God again for the first time. And all I asked him was what I did wrong. His response was, *'Nothing, but fear not—for He is with me. That He will strengthen me and help me and will uphold me with the right hand of His righteousness.'*

"I knew God had a plan, but at that time, it felt too overwhelming for a young woman like myself. Soon, I felt that suicidal feeling vanish, and peace replaced it. I even looked better for the hospital to discharge me.

"That was when I called Dad again. He sounded better, and I knew he was telling me the truth when he said that he had gotten right again with the Lord and was praying for God to heal us as a family. He could never tell a lie; it was not his nature.

"He told me he missed me and how much he

loved me—that made me cry. And when he heard me crying, he started crying as well. It was then that I told him I missed him but that I wasn't ready to return home yet.

"I have been on the streets since because I couldn't trust being around people. I slept in buildings and searched for food through garbage to avoid people in fear of being raped or beaten again. But I found that I was conversing more with God since I had no one else to talk to, and He started to comfort me with his words. It was what kept me going.

"It was the Lord who told me to trust you that day when I told you I would go with you. I felt scared, too, and was so hesitant in obeying him, but I was so tired of being out there, alone," she concluded.

Brady pulled her into his arms, giving her the love and support she needed. He, too, had missed so much in his life, but all that he had, he gave to her.

For the first time in her life since leaving her dad, Sara felt safe with a man; she allowed Brady to comfort her. It wasn't anything he did that impressed upon her in trusting him with her past. It was her growing relationship with the Lord over the past two years that helped her recognise His voice clearly, giving her the faith to trust Brady.

She wrapped her arms around his waist and let go of it all. A weight lifted from her entire body that had been weighing down on her for so long.

By this time, it was way down into the evening, almost 6:00 p.m. The sun curtsied beneath the trees, and the moon came to take its place, casting a reflection on the river. Hunger came over them; they got up to prepare dinner.

Brady and Sara were now thankful to have each other in their lives, even as friends, to help them face their past demons and move forward.

CHAPTER 12- A MOMENT OF GRATITUDE

"Sara, can I help you prepare the lasagne today?" Brady asked as they walked into the kitchen.

She smiled, appreciating his kind gesture. "I would like that very much, Brady."

"What can I do?"

"Take the mincemeat out of the fridge. Let's add some seasoning to it before we start to cook it."

"Got it," Brady smiled with enthusiasm and walked towards the fridge.

Sara stared at him, and she beamed with gratitude to God. She had obeyed God's voice when He told her to trust Brady, and in doing so, she had felt safe enough to trust Brady with her past. With the weight of it now lifted from her shoulders, peace enveloped her.

Even the barriers she had placed around herself as a shield from being hurt by men were soon to fade. She felt a lot more relaxed around Brady, which allowed them to worked together preparing dinner.

Once the meal was done, they sat and enjoyed it with laughter in the air. After dinner, Brady showed her around the living room and introduced all his family members to her from the many photos that decorated the room. Sara walked over to the piano and sat, then called Brady to sit next to her.

"Brady, do you have a favourite song? Something that brings you to a place where nothing dark or sad can creep in?" Sara asked, looking deep into his green eyes.

It took Brady a few minutes to recall if he did. Lexington didn't give its inmates life's pleasure to live like normal human beings until they'd proven that they could be civil and get along with others.

Then, even then, the musical options were not so great. It was just enough to allow them to keep their sanity while living in such isolation, as visitors were not allowed. It was one of the strategies the prison board took in trying to reform prisoners.

A faint smile spread across Brady's face while he searched through his memory. "I think I can remember one that was special to my mum. It became a favourite of mine, too. Each time I find myself singing it, I would always have a flashback of seeing Mum, where she's singing and dancing to it in the kitchen while she prepared dinner. It got me through many dark days while in Lexington. Hold on," he said, his eyes combing the room.

Sara watched him traverse to the opposite side of the room and retrieved a guitar from behind an armchair, which stood by itself in the corner.

"This was where Gram used to sit and read us Bible stories." Brady sank into the chair and stared at Sara. "Gram made everything fun, even when she used to call us into the kitchen to help her bake her tasty pies." He began to strum the guitar. "Do you want to hear the song? My mum wrote it, so you would not have heard it anywhere. It was her dream to write and sing worship songs—I think it was even I who ruined that dream for her, too."

"Brady, I would love to hear it," Sara interjected in a soft voice to prevent him from spiralling down into a guilt trip and into depression. A smile came across his face, and he began to sing.

1.
When the life that you're living seems to grow worse every day.
And you're looking for a way to take the hurt and pain away.
When the people you've been trusting in, to help to build you up,
Turns around and breaks your spirit and rob you of your joy.

Chorus.
Think about the one called Jesus.
Who was bruised for your sins, left his throne in glory to take away your hurt?
He was rejected by the very people he came

to save.
Yet He fulfilled his purpose and gave us the gift to love unconditionally.

2.

Sometimes you feel you have no control over your life.
And the more you try to break free from the struggles, the deeper you fall
Just reach for the hand of the one who gave His life for you
And look towards the light beyond the darkness.

Bridge.
His arms are open and waiting to embrace you.
To dry your tears and fill your heart with peace.
Only He can save you, only He can heal you, only His love is perfect and true.
Call out to Jesus and feel His spirit; He comes to fill you with His love.
Life is precious, and so are you.
God loves me, and He loves you too.
So be strong in the Lord and the power of His might.
Have faith and let His love for you be your saving grace.
Because Jesus's love is the only love you need.
Because Jesus's love is the only love you need.

Sara watched him as he sang with such

passion, and she felt butterflies dancing inside her stomach. His voice sounded so rich, and the words felt like they were meant just for her. She could see how such a song could be a tower of strength for him in his darkest moments.

She found herself smiling throughout the entire song. Each time she was around him, he kept on surprising her. She found that she wanted so much to embrace life and see how she could contribute something good to it. Brady motivated her without even knowing it.

By the end of the song, Sara watched as Brady's face grew red, and she wasn't sure what to make of it. He also grew a bit shy around her, and she wondered why. She didn't have much experience with men in a proper relationship. She was clueless about what each gesture meant, and she was afraid to ask. Brady replaced the guitar behind the chair.

"Brady, can you place the guitar next to the piano here, so we can play together sometimes? Music is great therapy, you know," she remarked. "Come and sit back next to me for a bit—I have a surprise for you," she added with a soft smile after he placed the guitar next to the piano.

Brady sat next to her and smiled, eager to know what her surprise was. Sara turned her attention to the piano and started playing a piece she created. Brady thought he had heard all she played and wondered when she created this piece.

It was filled with such softness, almost as if you could feel the tenderness of someone's love and appreciation towards you. While she played, he kept his eyes on her and wondered if she was somehow purposed to be in his life, even though it was he who asked God to be of help to her. He felt like she was a part of him already, and she was bringing out such strange, unfamiliar feelings in him.

"Thank you so much for that, Sara. I appreciated it very much. That's the nicest thing anyone has done for me since Gram. I started to think I would never be good enough to receive such kindness from anyone again," he almost choked on his words.

"I just wanted to tell you I am grateful for all you have done for me, Brady. And also give you something to maybe help you sleep well tonight," she reached over and hugged him.

He allowed her to comfort him as he had done for her earlier. He didn't feel so alone anymore. "Let's go watch some TV before we go to bed since it's still early. What do you say?"

"I'd like that."

As they sat on the couch, Brady switched on the television and then stared at Sara. "What do we watch? All they allowed us to watch in Lexington were comedies and dramas. They feared action movies would make us resort to violence, and they wanted to have that under control—no romance either for fear of a homosexual outbreak," he chuckled. "So, you choose what we watch," he suggested.

Sara laughed, then took the remote and began flicking through the channels.

CHAPTER 13- FACING MY DEMONS

Brady and Sara settled on a movie called Rocky, and by the end of the movie, both were exhausted. They dragged themselves up the stairs and into their respective bedrooms after saying goodnight to each other. Sara was out the minute her head hit the soft pillows, of which she could not get enough.

Brady also fell asleep right away, but a constant banging caused him to jump up from his sleep after an hour. The moonlight, which shone into his darkened room, drew his eyes to the window. He wrapped his thick covers around himself and ambled over to the window to secure the latch, which had been left open, then dragged himself back over to his bed. Falling back onto his pillows, he tossed from left to right, growing quite restless as sleep failed to return.

Memories he had long suppressed

bombarded his mind, giving him an instant headache. He pressed his hands against his temples, trying to force out the throbbing pain.

You've been running too long, Brady. It's time to face your demons and release them for good. He heard that inner voice tell him.

"I avoided them because they were too hard to deal with. I don't know if I want to relive all that pain when my life now seems to be better," he responded.

For the plans I have for you, you have to face them and not be affected by them anymore, that inner voice spoke again.

Brady settled on his back and stared up at the ceiling, allowing his mind to search back to see where it all had started to go downhill. As the images came into a clearer focus, he shut his eyes tight, almost afraid to embark on the journey. But just as quickly, the same inner voice whispered, *remember, I have not given you a spirit of fear.*

"Poor Mum, I never made it easy for her, did I? She tried so hard and never showed how much she was suffering. *God, . . . if I go on this journey, please help me let go of the guilt that I have held on to for so many years, and help me to forgive myself,*" he prayed.

As Brady reflected on his past, his mind went as far back to his final year in high school, when he'd been expelled and found himself in an alley. He had been crying out to God to help him overcome the pain of John's death and also for him not to be such a burden and disappointment to his mother.

A girl about his age had shown up, stooped

down next to him, and tapped his shoulder, causing him to look up.

"I can help you forget the pain," she told him.

At that moment, it did not matter to him that he did not know her; all he cared about was getting rid of the pain, so he accepted her help.

His first encounter with drugs truly freed him from the pain and the hurt. However, his sheltered life did not prepare him for what would also end up becoming his nightmare. Soon, the urge for more drugs came, and it caused him to develop a nervous itch that he found hard to get rid of.

All the traumatic memories of John's death soon faded, as he was now faced with fighting another battle. Within a short space of time, his mother, Claudette, noticed his strange behaviour and insisted he see a doctor. He did not put up a fight; he felt like he was losing control of who he was, and he felt very afraid. He wanted to be there for her, too. The doctor confirmed that he had drugs in his system and advised his mum to get him into rehab.

Brady sighed and removed his gaze from the ceiling. He looked over to the moonlit window.

Two months after his seventeenth birthday, halfway into his senior year, his mum had advised his school of him going into rehab. There, she learned of his expulsion. Her pained expression upon confronting him left him disappointed.

Instead of getting upset, she sat him down and shared a solution: completing rehab, then taking extra classes to complete his GED to later join the Navy, as he and John had wanted. At that moment, nausea struck him. He not only felt he let her down but John as well.

He remembered the hopeful look on his mum's face when he kissed her on the cheek before he walked into the rehab facility. He promised he would come back and be there for her. Tears streamed down Brady's face as he recalled how he had utterly broken that promise. He had fought hard not to, but rehab turned out to be harder than he had imagined.

Going through the withdrawal stages at the facility brought out such rage in him. He knocked over one of the treatment nurses, who attended to him one evening and escaped. For two whole days, he hid from the world, sweating profusely and getting agitated.

Each time he saw John, he watched him fade in the distance without so much as a word. When he could not endure the aches and pains any longer, he found his way back home. The sight of him almost gave Claudette a nervous breakdown. She had been so scared when the rehab centre called and informed her that she called all the friends she knew and started praying, asking God to keep him safe.

The tears in his mother's eyes as she stood in the doorway, staring at him, seemed a memory he would never forget. She was not even angry by his actions at the rehab centre. She just pulled him into her arms and hugged him as her tears kept falling.

Later, she called the rehab centre, apologising to the doctors, letting them know he was home and okay. Claudette even helped him bathe and made him something to eat that night.

As soon as he was calm and relaxed, he made a promise to her that he would go back and complete his treatment, which he remembered made her smile.

Because he had managed to stay clean for the next few weeks, he did not see the reason to return to rehab, even against his mum's better judgement advising him to return. He thought he had it all under control and did not want to go through that difficult process again.

Wanting to redeem himself in both his brother's and his mum's eyes, he went ahead and searched for jobs and also registered for evening classes. He soon found work at a food store and, for the first few weeks, was doing well until he started catching a glimpse of a Navy-sponsored ad that repeated for a few days during his shift.

At first, he felt proud, knowing he would soon be able to fulfil what he and John wanted to do together—but then an eerie voice would creep up on him and whisper in his ears things that made him cover his ears each time.

You're nothing but a failure—a disappointment; second best to a brother, who was on top in everything.

For a couple of days, he managed to ignore the jeering voice until it became unbearable, and he would grab whatever drugs from the pharmaceutical section of the food store to drown out the voice.

Soon, he was exposed by one of his co-workers. An argument ensued when he lied and became defensive. This caused his temper to flare up; he pushed the young man, causing him to get fired on the spot.

In three places, the same thing happened. By this time, he had lost control of his cravings, and his final experience landed him in jail after he punched the boss in the face, breaking his nose. Mr. Santiago, his former boss, was not such a hard man, but the level of rage he saw coming from Brady brought so much fear in the poor man that he pressed charges. He thought Brady should be put away and given anger management treatment and counselling.

The judge, after seeing Brady, had some leniency towards him after Claudette pleaded on his behalf.

"Get him into an anger management class and some therapy as well. I will give you the addresses of some I recommend. If I see him here for this kind of misdemeanour again, your tears won't save him, and I will put him in a juvenile facility until he turns eighteen," the judge cautioned her. "And get him into rehab!" the judge shouted, getting her point across.

They thanked the judge. Once back at home, they sat in the living room, pondering what to do.

"Brady, why don't you go to visit your dad? You know how much he loves his boys and, seeing that you're all he has left, I think seeing each other would do you both some good," Claudette had suggested.

Thinking about his dad made him think his mum might have a good idea. His dad had always been the strict one, and since he needed to go back to rehab, he knew his father's firmness would motivate him to complete the programme.

"I think you're right, Mum," he told her, and it pleased her, causing her to kiss his cheek.

"You can even help your dad out at his hardware store and finish your classes there. That would make him so proud, you know," Claudette added.

"Mum, I love you. I know that I have hurt you since John died, but it has been hard facing life with him. He always knew how to deal with everything."

"Brady, John just matured early; you will get there, too. We all have to face life and learn how to make good decisions. Your brother always saw himself as the one to take care of us ever since your dad left. I told him to just enjoy becoming a teen and let me worry about us, but that didn't stop him, and I admired his spirit," she told him while she caressed his cheek.

"I will do my best, Mum." Brady kissed her cheek and hugged her.

Brady sat up in bed, trying to process the memories that came. He tossed his cover aside and got off the bed, then began to pace up and down in his room. That was the last good conversation he realised he had had with his mother.

After pacing the room for a few minutes, he walked over to the window and stared out into the quiet night. Tonight was one of the quietest nights he could recall in a long time of being at his grandmother's house.

Not even the sound of the noisome tadpoles that came out at night or the screeching owls that chimed in their creepy melody made a peep. Anyone not accustomed to the sounds of country life would find it haunting. It was as if everything in nature decided to help him focus, staying silent so his thoughts could flow freely without their constant distractions.

"I will make you proud, Mum. This time, I will keep my promise to you," he said to himself just before another surge of memories flooded his mind.

CHAPTER 14- BRADY AND HIS DAD

Frank was all smiles when he picked Brady up at the airport in Miami and gave him a big hug. Although he was not one to shed tears, he never shied away from giving or receiving hugs. He had decided the year John died that a change of scenery was what he needed and had moved to Miami, which to him proved to be the perfect escape.

Brady felt so delighted to see his dad, and like Frank, the change of scenery felt refreshing. He called his mum the minute they got to his father's house, and she enlightened Frank about all she and Brady had discussed—an idea Frank himself agreed with.

For the first few weeks, everything went well. Brady even got along with his stepmother, Denise. He never forgot how she had helped his dad with John's funeral arrangements and even came all the way out to his grandmother's for the burial. His grandfather made sure he had bought land not too far from the house to serve as a burial ground for the family.

With the encouragement he got from Frank, he completed his extra classes to get his GED within three months and his rehab treatments. He found he was even enthusiastic while preparing for the exams. The look of joy on his mum's face when he presented his high school certificate to her was always visual in his mind. He had met a few friends since he came to Miami, most of whom were from his classes, but his dad was always like his Jiminy Cricket.

"Brady, please be careful with those new friends of yours."

He knew his dad meant well—not wanting to see him go into another relapse, and he appreciated his dad's effort in helping him stay on the right path. For that reason, he never argued when Frank warned him about some of his potential friends.

Most weekends, his friends would invite him to parties. Even though he was seventeen and knew he was almost at the age to make his own decisions, he always asked his dad for his input. He wanted to stay clean, especially living in a new city—being an addict wasn't who he wanted to be again. He hated the act of injecting drugs into his body, which was to be kept clean—*a temple for the Lord,* as his grandmother and his mum always told him and John.

Each week, he would call his mum and keep her updated on his progress. She was so excited when she heard he had completed his rehab programme and was now studying for his GED exam. Brady had now spent a little over three months in Miami. He felt nervous as he and Frank stood outside the examination room entrance.

"Brady, my son, look how far you have come. I am very proud of you, and so would John be if he was here," Frank encouraged him just before he pulled him into a fatherly hug. "I love you, Son. Now go, do your best."

"Thank you, Dad."

Three weeks later, Brady, his dad, and Denise celebrated after receiving the letter from the examination board, showing he had passed with very high scores. Both his mum and grandmother were excited when they got the phone call about his accomplishment. Frank was so happy that he cried at seeing his son happy again after everything that happened since John's death.

Brady's friends, who did the exam with him and also did well, thought this should count for him going out and celebrating with them. This time, Frank agreed. They went to a house party. Brady and his friends walked out onto the dance floor and danced hard, not caring what other dancers thought of their dance moves.

He drank a few beers when his friends handed out rounds while they all were laughing and enjoying themselves. Amid their celebration, a beautiful young woman, dancing not too far from them, caught Brady's eyes. With his friend's encouragement, he walked over to her and asked her to dance, and she accepted, much to his delight.

"Ouch!" Brady yelled from the impact of his fist slamming into the wall when his mind began to enter parts of his memories he regretted.

He had left the dance floor and his friends, following that girl—the beautiful and seductive Maria. She took his hand, swayed her hips, and led him out into the courtyard, where they found a bench and sat down.

Finding himself overcome by teenage passion—or lust if you will—he tried to kiss and fondle her. She moaned with pleasure while she searched for something in her pockets. Soon, she pulled out a marijuana joint. At the sight of it, Brady backed away and got up. He was about to leave when she pulled him back and kissed him hard. Soon, he found himself lost in her kisses.

"Don't worry, Brady, it's not coke. I would not give any to you, knowing you had a problem with it before. I have been smoking this for two years, and it has not affected me negatively; otherwise, I would not use it. And, hey, you must have heard it has medicinal benefits, too," she tempted him. She took a puff and blew out the smoke, almost in a seductive matter.

As Brady sat there, he thought of the couple of times he had seen her before. She had always looked upbeat. With that conclusion, he took it from her hand and took a long pull on the joint, choking as the smoke met his throat. By the time they both finished smoking, their sexual urges were in high gear. Soon, they found a room, the seductress, Maria, gave him a condom, and they had sex.

A bang on the door brought them out of their state of ecstasy. It was the sound of his friends telling him they were ready to leave. After both he and his temptress got dressed, she wrote her name and number on a piece of paper and tucked it into his jeans pocket.

His first major party, and boy did he have fun. He had gotten the number of a girl who he had been admiring for weeks since coming to Miami. She told him she was glad he approached her, as she had found him very handsome.

"Seductive Maria was my downfall," Brady lamented as he continued, staring out his room window.

By the time he had gotten home that night, it was around 2:00 a.m., and out of concern, Frank had waited up for him. Happy to see him back and okay, Frank breathed a sigh of relief. He pulled Brady into a hug but then suddenly withdrew.

"Are you high?" His voice grew harsh and his face serious.

"Come on, Dad, I'm fine," Brady answered, smiling from ear to ear, and walked past him, going into the living room.

Frank became furious as he marched behind Brady. "I can smell the stench of marijuana on you. How can you be so reckless, knowing even *that* can be addictive?" His voice grew louder.

"Dad! It was just one smoke, and I am not planning to start using drugs anytime soon," Brady replied defensively. "And what's the big deal? Isn't marijuana legal now because of its health benefits?" he said before he shrugged.

Frank's hand went hard against Brady's cheek, causing Brady to rub his throbbing cheek and glared at Frank as his temper now heightened.

"Dad, you slapped me for that! I have never disrespected you before, and yet you raised your hand and hit me. Is that the only way you know how to get your point across! I can now see where I got my temper from," Brady yelled.

He turned his back to Frank and stepped towards the front door. Frank pulled him back by his collar.

"Where do you think you're going?" Frank barked at him.

"Anywhere from here!" Brady snapped. "I need some space to breathe." He yanked his shirt from his father's grip, but Frank held on firmly. Brady felt his breathing intensifying and his heart pounding hard in his chest. With one hard swing backwards, his elbow thwacked hard into Frank's chest, causing Frank to stagger back and release him.

Brady took two steps towards the door, but Frank lunged at him and locked his right elbow around his neck.

"Do you think you're man enough to challenge me?" Frank said harshly.

Brady twisted in Frank's grip, trying to free himself. When he found Frank's grip was too strong, he stomped his heels one by one onto Franks' feet. Frank yelped and tried to maintain his hold on Brady but had to release him when Brady applied more pressure, pressed his heels once more onto Frank's feet.

Once he was free, he swung around and landed a punch on his father's cheek, only to be met by one into his gut. He groaned but didn't relent, not wanting his father to feel any satisfaction.

He grabbed Frank and pushed him against the wall, slamming his fist into Frank's ribs. Frank returned with even more force. The commotion was so loud it caused Denise to rush from the bedroom in fright.

Even though scared to get between two strong-bodied men, Denise grabbed a mop and began hitting them hard on their heads, causing them to let go of each other and shield themselves. It was then that Brady managed to slip away out of the house.

CHAPTER 15- VENTING FRUSTRATIONS

Brady stomped his way down the steps of his father's house, flung the gate open, and kicked over every trashcan that stood along his father's street. When he got to the end of the street, he took a deep breath and then let out a loud groan, like a wounded animal.

Rage consumed him, unlike any he had ever felt since John's death. His father's inability to trust him to make a decision that would not ruin his life left him wounded. After all, he knew how much his mother needed him, and he didn't plan on letting marijuana ruin his life like how drugs almost did.

Brady flipped up his jacket collar to protect his neck from the chill in the air and wandered around the city in the cold dead of the night. After a couple of minutes passed, he realised he was lost. All that rage coursing through him caused him to take a wrong turn in an unpleasant part of town. He noticed most of the buildings in this area stood abandoned, with a few warehouses along its path. Not a vehicle in sight, except for those that were now scrapped, most of which had no wheels or windows.

There was an eeriness about the area, but Brady felt no fear, even when he spotted two Hispanic-looking men sitting on top of an old run-down truck a few yards from him. They stared with fierce eyes while passing a joint back and forth between them. Seeing that joint only infuriated Brady more, reminding him of what transpired earlier with his dad.

He quickened his pace towards them. In his mind, if it was to be his last night, then so be it; he wasn't going without a fight after all he had already suffered in his life. Someone would get the end result of all the anger and frustration he was feeling up to that point.

As he neared the two men, he watched as the older-looking one draw from the joint before he flicked it away. Then he slid off the truck with the younger man following behind him. He stepped in front of Brady, barring his way with a sinister smile on his face, and flipped out his switchblade. His friend mimicked his every move. Brady stopped and stared at them with narrowed eyes.

The first man was tall and slender, about six feet, two inches with white complexion. He looked to be in his early twenties and had a tattoo, which covered the entire left side of his neck. He had a military-style haircut and a fierce look, which hid his seldom handsome features.

The second guy was of brown complexion and looked to be around the same age, height and built as Brady, who stood at six feet, athletic, and weighed 175 lbs. This guy, however, carried a fearless attitude. He was quite the handsome fellow, but the hostility and anger seen in his eyes would easily scare women away, unaware when he would snap. Brady felt as if he saw a reflection of himself while he stared at the young man.

The two men stared at Brady, giving him the impression they thought him loaded with cash because he dressed in nicely fitted blue jeans, a white dress shirt, a black jacket, and new sneakers.

Brady smiled, causing the men to look at each other puzzled, then back at him with caution, wondering what he was up to. Slowly and very carefully, he went into his jeans pocket and took out the cash he had left, and thrown it on the ground in front of them, watching for them to pick it up. The younger man reached for the money while the other kept his eyes fixed on Brady, who still had a smile on his face.

"Your watch," the older man said to him, his knife pointed towards Brady.

"You and your comrade have knives; why don't one of you cut it off my hand?" Brady replied nonchalantly.

"Drop it!" the man shouted. "Aren't you afraid of dying, man?" he uttered, straight-faced.

"Nope. If you are here to do so, you better get started; I'm already in a very bad mood. I don't think it's going away soon," Brady told them, leaving the two men in a state of confusion as his smile faded.

Infuriated with Brady's stubbornness, the older man rushed towards him and slashed him across his left shoulder with his blade. Brady moved with such quick precision, he kicked the man's feet off the ground, causing him to fall flat onto his back. His knife fell a few feet from them both. Brady jumped down on the man and started punching him senseless.

With each punch, it was like releasing all his anger and frustration—from losing his only brother and best friend, John, who was always good to everyone, to becoming a victim of something as nasty as drugs, and now his dad's lack of faith in believing that he was capable of handling himself.

Brady's weight upon the man and the strength of his punches did not give the man room to defend himself. Almost at the point of unconsciousness, he called to his friend for help. The younger man rushed to his friend's aid, kneeing Brady's face in, knocking him over and off his friend, pulling him up to his feet.

It seemed like the Hulk had now come out in full rage. Within a few seconds, Brady was up on his feet and rushed towards the two men. He grabbed hold of the younger man, swinging the man around, thrusting a hard blow to his cheek. This allowed the very badly beaten man to escape for his life.

Somehow, the younger man had misplaced his knife when he went to help his friend, which caused him and Brady to vent out their rage towards each other the good old-fashioned way. He was just as fierce as Brady was, both throwing hard blows at each other. They were so enraged with each other that the sounds of the approaching police car did not stop them from pounding on each other.

With very bloody faces, swollen eyes, cheeks, and bruised ribs, neither now had the strength to run when two patrolling police officers approached and started pulling them off each other.

One of the police officers, who knew first-aid, had noticed the wound and applied bandages to Brady's arm before throwing him and the other young man into the back of the police car.

"It's such a shame that young men nowadays can't find better ways to solve their conflicts rather than busting each other's faces like these two idiots," one of the officers said to the other as they drove the two young men to the station.

"I agree. I seriously hope no one turns up to bail them tonight so they can cool off and get their acts together," the other replied harshly while eyeing the boys as they sat quietly in the back seats, both looking out their respective windows.

With all the adrenaline coursing through Brady when he withstood the older of his two adversaries, the searing of the knife wound did not faze him even as the blood soaked through his shirt until now.

Upon entering the station, one of the police officers glanced up at the station's clock—it was now 4 a.m.

"Sit on that bench over there, you two, while we figure out what to do with you!" he said to them in a harsh tone.

The boys complied, both feeling too worn out to stir any further trouble. The two officers walked to their desks and let out a long sigh after sitting down.

"What do you think, Charles? Should we call those boys' parents at this hour just to let them come bail them after the state we found them?" The first officer said.

"Why?" Charles scoffed. "Let the poor parents enjoy their sleep. What normal kids would be out on the street in such an isolated area at that ungodly hour? They probably torment their parents and have no respect for them either. Bob, I suggest we throw them in a cell with all the roughnecks to teach them a lesson—it might show them the future that awaits them if they continue on this path."

Bob chuckled. "I think you are right, Charles; when Serge comes on duty later, we will update him of the situation. You know his ideas for such troubled teens; he'll know what to do with them."

Charles snickered at Bob's remark. "You are so right; I wouldn't want to be in their shoes. I'll take them around back." He rose, walked around the counter, and stood in front of the boys, who stared up at him with defeated looks on their faces.

"What's your names?"

"Brady O'Connor."

"Shawn Garcia."

"Okay, on your feet and follow me," Officer Charles commanded.

Brady and Shawn dragged their limping bodies behind Officer Charles knowing where they were heading. Brady had never spent a night in jail before, and glancing over at Shawn, he doubted Shawn had either. After watching the officer open the cell door, neither boy made any effort to move.

"Get in there!" Officer Charles sneered at them and shoved them inside the cell.

The vicious stares from the other prisoners kept them alert and ready for anything. Although exhausted, both carefully walked to an isolated corner. The pain from the beatings they had inflicted on each other started kicking in.

As they sat on the floor of the cell with their backs pressed against the hard wall, they could hardly keep their eyes open. They fought hard to stay awake, confined with all those fierce-looking prisoners—some of whom looked to be murderers. None of the men seemed to be remorseful for whatever brought them in there.

It was one of the longest nights for Brady and Shawn.

CHAPTER 16- BIRDS OF A FEATHER

"Wake up, you two!" Officer Bob, yelled as he spun the key into the lock. Shawn and Brady scrambled to their feet and limped their way over to the cell door. Bob pulled open the steel door and tilted his head in the direction of the station room. "Move it!" he added with piercing eyes.

After booking them and getting their guardians' contact information, Officer Bob had them sit and wait. Now that the effects of the night before had worn off, looking at them could have fooled anyone into believing they were just normal-looking teens that had a bit too much to drink.

Officer Bob nudged the sergeant, who had now started his shift, to look over at the two boys. They now sat, quite unruffled, as they waited for their relatives to show up. Both men shook their heads as they wondered what could possess normal teens to become as violent as these two were earlier that morning.

Forty-five minutes later, two new officers came into the station and walked up to the desk where Officer Bob and the sergeant stood working. The shorter of the two leant against the counter and stared at the boys. "Is that them?" he asked in a husky tone, causing Brady and Shawn to stare back at him with curious eyes.

"Yes. Take them to the hospital to get treated—I need to make sure they did not permanently damage each other. Don't let them out of your sight and bring them back here as soon as the doctor is done with them," the sergeant commanded.

"We're not getting bailed out today," Shawn whispered with his eyes fixed on the sergeant and the officers.

Brady turned his attention to Shawn for a moment, surprised that he spoke to him. "How do you know that?" he asked, then turned his eyes back to the officers.

"I just do," Shawn replied and said nothing else.

The two new officers collected the paperwork from the sergeant and marched towards Brady and Shawn.

"Up on your feet!" the short one commanded.

The boys hauled themselves out of the station as their sore bruises ached.

At the hospital, the doctor assigned them beds next to each other.

"I will be with you boys in a few minutes," the doctor spoke gently. He then turned to the officers. "I have an agitated patient who seems to only respond to me. Right now, I need to calm him down so we can administer his treatment," he added and rushed off.

The officers looked at each other and then at the two young men in front of them. Then, like some secret language spoken between them with no words, the officers moved towards Brady and Shawn's bed, handcuffed one of their hands to their bedposts, then stood back with folded arms, eyes fixed on them.

Brady and Shawn kept silent while the officers stood, staring at them. The beds seemed more appealing to them at that moment. They both just fell back and closed their eyes.

After a couple of minutes, the doctor returned. "Wow, they must have been really tired," he chuckled. Then his brows creased in confusion, and he turned to the officers. "Were they handcuffed before I left the first time?"

"No, they weren't, Doc," the taller officer responded, straight-faced with a baritone voice.

"But don't let their pretty boy innocent looks fool you," the shorter officer chipped in. "After we heard you talk about the patient you tended to, we remembered the report we got on these two," he said, eyes growing mean, "let's just say *we're being cautious*, Doc."

"Alright," the doctor responded and walked over to their beds. He went to Shawn first and examined him. The minute he touched Shawn's ribs, the young man's eyes flew open, and he groaned. "Young man, you have a few bruised ribs but no permanent damage. I am going to give you something for the pain, dress that cut over your eye, and put a cold compress on your cheek to get the swelling down."

Shawn groaned in response and closed his eyes again. Brady was still asleep while the doctor treated Shawn. The throbbing pain from the knife wound tormented him while he slept. He soon jumped up from his sleep, feeling confused.

"Aww, he's awake," the doctor turned his attention to Brady. He placed a thermometer into Brady's mouth to check his temperature. After he removed it and read it, he said, "Son, I have to give you an injection before I dress that wound."

The doctor removed the old bandage that the officer had applied and then flicked his fingers against the syringe. Brady turned his head away when the doctor pierced his skin with the needle.

"Ouch!" he yelled and glared at the doctor.

"How can you be scared of a tiny needle like this?" the doctor asked with a chuckle.

Brady did not respond. He glanced over at Shawn, who had gone back to sleep, then returned his gaze to the doctor. "Doctor, can you give me something for this pain?" he groaned, pointing to his chest.

"Sure I will. You are lucky that you didn't get any major damage done to your ribs. The bruises will heal in a couple of days. Try not to get into any more fights, alright?" the doctor encouraged. Brady nodded.

As soon as the doctor finished administering Brady's dressings and gave him the pain medication, Brady fell back onto the pillow and closed his eyes. The doctor walked over to the officers and placed his hands into his shirt pocket.

"I have given them some pain medication. It will keep them asleep for at least four hours; their bodies badly need the rest. They are not fit to go back to a cell in their condition yet. When they awake, you can take them back to the station. I will go prepare the paperwork and be back once I'm finished."

By the time the boys left the hospital, they felt a lot better, wearing downcast faces as they headed back to jail. Both wondered if either of their families had shown up, eager to take them back home. Brady wondered if his dad was still in a bad mood from the night before.

He knew his father had a short temper, which was why he and his mother had gotten a divorce. However, since he had been to Miami, last night was the first time he had seen his dad's temper resurface. Brady thought maybe his father would by now have cooled down. By the time they returned to the station, it was past 1:00 p.m. No sign of their relatives.

"Bring them here!" the sergeant told the officers. As the boys approached the front desk, a bad feeling fell to the pit of their stomachs. "Your families came today while you were at the hospital and were told that you will not be getting bail today."

"What!" both interrupted him in unison, then stared at each other before returning their eyes to the sergeant.

With a serious look on his face, the sergeant continued. "As I was saying, your behaviour early this morning is very disturbing and dangerous. We found a knife on the scene of your altercation, and that makes me believe that it's not safe to release you two back into your homes as you are. Therefore, I have sent your case to Judge Ryan, who will decide what to do with you two upon seeing you boys tomorrow. I suggest you use the time inside the cell to think well and hard about where you want to see your lives going from here," he concluded. "Escort these two back with the others," he said to one of the officers.

Both boys didn't bother arguing with the sergeant. They obediently followed the officer, who led them back into the cell before removing their cuffs. As much as they felt torn inside, they kept their composure as to not show any level of fear among the other prisoners, who stared at them with unreadable eyes.

Though they almost killed each other earlier that morning, it seemed that each other was all they had right now. With no spoken words, they stuck by each other as they previously did when they first came in. Later that evening, the officers sent in food for the prisoners, and as the two boys ate, they kept watch for the others. They managed to sleep without being harassed by other prisoners.

The next day came. Both boys were awake before an officer came to serve them something to eat. They were to be at the courthouse at noon. Within two hours before that, they were taken to the shower room, where they were allowed to shower and change into the fresh clothes their families had brought the day before.

Now, standing in the courtroom facing the judge, they felt remorseful for their actions. They saw their families sitting behind them, looking displeased, which made them feel even worse.

"Shawn Garcia, you're back again," the stern middle-aged judge began, looking hard at the young man. "This is your third time here, and each time, it's the same offence: fights and weapons. Don't you have anything you want to live for that will motivate you to stop this madness?" Judge Ryan shouted harshly at him, frustrated.

The judge frowned and took a deep breath. He glanced over at Shawn's aunt, who had now turned her gaze to Shawn, and he saw the frustrated look on the poor woman's face.

Judge Ryan looked back at Shawn and saw the disappointment on his aunt's face reflect onto Shawn's.

"This is my judgement for you," Judge Ryan continued. "Since you're going to be eighteen in about seven months, I am going to place you in a juvenile facility. I hope you will get your act together there. Your aunt looks like she needs a break from all your madness, and she might have some peace of mind knowing that you will be someplace where they can keep an eye on you and not someplace where you might likely end up dead in a ditch somewhere. *Look at me, Shawn*," the judge said now in a softer tone.

"I know you had problems with your dad. But everyone in life has difficulties. If we all act out like you, we'd all be locked up. Please . . . I know it's hard but try to use the time inside to think about what you can do in your future to help your mother and aunt, alright?" the judge advised him with much concern.

"Yes, Sir," Shawn replied, almost at the brink of tears as he looked back at his aunt.

As Brady listened to the judge talk to Shawn, he was surprised; he had thought he was the only one with big problems. Now he felt a bit sympathetic towards Shawn.

"Now you, Brady O'Connor!" he heard the judge shout at him, bringing his focus to the very stern judge. "Although it's your first time here, I have received reports of your mischief back in Philadelphia. The last presiding judge that looked at your case wrote in her report that if you showed up again, you, too, will end up in a juvenile facility. I see in her report that your temper is out of control that needs controlling. I am also making the same ruling for you as I have for Mr. Garcia since you are also the same age," he sighed.

"I spoke to your father just before we started, and he shared the same sentiments as I have ruled here today. And upon leaving here, you and Mr. Garcia will be placed in the St. Peter's Juvenile Facility. You'll stay there until you reach eighteen."

With that ruling, the judge banged his gavel and dismissed the court. He allowed them to say goodbye to their family before they were escorted to St. Peter's Juvenile Facility. Brady did not even bother turning to look at his dad. He was too hurt and disappointed by his dad's lack of faith to believe that he had changed. Denise gave him a hug and a word of encouragement. He could hear his dad's angry voice calling her to leave, and she shot him an angry look and continued to hug Brady.

"Don't worry, Brady; I will call you as often as I can, and if I can visit, I will. I know you were doing your best. Your father can't let go of things easily, so give him time. He will soon come around. I know I may not be your mum, but I care a lot for you, too, Brady," she smiled and caressed his cheek.

"My mum . . . Gram," he said, stifling a tear.

"Oh, don't worry, I will explain everything to them so they won't be disappointed or mad at you. Your mother and your grandmother love you and will understand." Denise gave him a soft kiss on his cheek before she said goodbye.

Shawn's aunt, Marie, on the other hand, had mixed emotions about him going there. She wanted to be free of him because of his outlandish behaviour. She also wanted to keep him from harm and wondered if him going there would be better. She hugged him and kissed him on his cheeks.

"I'm sorry, Shawn. I did everything I could for you, knowing your mum can't care for you as she wants to. I think maybe God is intervening on my behalf for you right now. Sending you away for a while will help you come to terms with everything. Please, come back and help me care for your mum, okay? Even though she does not talk, she writes when she can, and she always writes things, saying I must take care of you. She is always thinking of you even as she is now."

Marie stifled a tear.

"Please, Aunt Marie, tell Mum I love her, okay? I will change. I promise."

Marie nodded.

Soon, Shawn and Brady were escorted out of the courtroom and onto a bus that would take them straight to St. Peter's, which was in another state.

CHAPTER 17- LIFE AT ST. PETER'S

The journey to St. Peter's Juvenile Detention Centre took approximately five hours. The sun's heat had the boys fanning themselves with their hands, and wiping their necks with their shirts. The hostility between them had somewhat died down, and together, they observed the scenery, which now guided them to their new home for the next seven months.

"I'm sorry, Brady, that my friend and I attacked you. We usually just rob people and let them go," Shawn apologised and stretched his hand over to Brady in hopes of making peace.

Brady studied him for a moment and saw the sincerity in his eyes.

"I'm sorry, too, Shawn," he responded with a smile and shook Shawn's hand. "My dad made me angry that night. We fought, and then I stormed out. I didn't even know where I was when I ended up in that part of town."

Both boys, who sat across from each other, now turned to face each other and conversed, being the only two passengers on the bus. The driver glanced up at his mirror every now and then to ensure they were behaving.

"Why were you and your dad fighting?" Shawn asked.

"He lost his temper because I smoked a joint at a party; I was a little high," Brady chuckled, then got serious and continued. "I mean, I know I had a drug problem before, and I know how damaging it was to both my mum and me. But I came to Miami and went through the whole programme, which I might add wasn't easy. I pushed and endured just to overcome it, and I did. That night you saw me, I had gone out and celebrated with my friends because we all passed our exams to get our GED. We were all high school dropouts."

"You had a drug problem? That is very serious stuff. I can see why your dad would be concerned," Shawn said surprisingly, causing Brady to glare at him. He raised his hands to surrender and continued. "Hey, I'm not picking sides, okay? I'm just saying that you and your dad shouldn't turn against each other because of that. But I get that you overcame it and thought that you could handle marijuana and felt that he should have had some faith in you."

"Yeah, he should. After all, I have proven to him that I am responsible. In fact, I asked for his opinion on everything I did just to keep myself from having another relapse. So, why couldn't he just let me enjoy the one night that I got to have some fun, especially after knowing how depressed I had been in the past?" Brady stressed.

"Fathers can be difficult at times and very unpredictable. Some don't even know how to express emotions, which is why many of them beat their wives and kids," Shawn added.

"Is that what happened with your dad?" Brady asked, now interested to know more about his new friend.

Shawn's countenance turned sad, and he almost did not answer but seeing Brady face some of what he did, he felt at ease sharing with him.

"Yes," he finally began, "he always came home drunk and beat up on my mum. Each time I tried to help her, I would end up getting some hard punches. That's where I developed that toughness. I hated him so much. I wanted to kill him myself every time I saw him abuse Mum. He never even seemed to have a reason to do it to her when he did. I asked him one time when he was sober if he beat her because he hated Mum. He burst into tears, knowing he did it. I could not understand the man. He loved her, yet he beat her, and she never wanted to involve the police. I begged her to move out, and she said he's still her husband."

"What happened to your mother to cause you to live with your aunt?"

Shawn almost broke into tears thinking about his mum. "She had a stroke and is in a nursing home now. Dad came home—drunk as always—and beat up Mum. I stepped in, as I usually do. He pulled a gun on me, threatening to shoot. The minute Mum heard those words, she collapsed and curled up on the floor. My dad panicked after seeing what he caused, and right there, he blew his brains out. You can see now why I am the way I am," he finished as the tears flowed, quickly wiping them away.

"No way! You're kidding, right!" Brady blurted, causing the driver to look around in fright. He sprang from his seat and stepped across to where Shawn sat. He plopped down next to him and gave him a manly hug.

"What's happening around there?" the driver shouted.

"It's okay, Sir, we're fine. My friend is just scared to go to a juvenile centre. He's never been away from his family before," Brady lied to the driver, then turned his attention to his friend again. "I'm sorry, Shawn, you and I truly are so much alike."

"Well, you boys should have thought about your attitudes before causing trouble for others if you're afraid of places like this," he spat back at them, having no remorse for them. "And you, get back to your seat!" he yelled at Brady.

"I'm okay, Brady, go back to your seat," Shawn advised him as his lips curled into a small smile. As Brady sat back across from him, he added, "Now that you know my story and I know yours—friends?"

"Yes, friends," Brady answered and smiled back.

When the bus came to a halt at its intended destination, the boys noticed a thick-bodied woman, who looked to be in her mid-forties standing outside the door. She had the look of someone in authority. Her face was firm but not harsh, and she held some paperwork in her hand.

"Your name and age?" the woman commanded as they stepped down from the bus.

After she ticked off their names, she began scrutinising them one after the other as if trying to match them up with the information she was now reading about them.

"Well," she began, "I am Superintendent Watkins, and I can tell you boys that I will not put up with any foolishness from either of you while you're staying here. And don't think," she stressed, "that I will hesitate in recommending you boys to be sent to the big house after staying here if I don't see improvements from what your reports say here. Now follow me," she warned.

Neither Shawn nor Brady spoke but quietly glanced at each other while the superintendent gave them her welcoming speech. As they followed her inside the facility, their hearts thudded as reality hit them. The facility looked a lot like an adult prison.

"We'll survive it here," Brady whispered to Shawn, seeing a look on Shawn's face that reflected what he felt.

Shawn glanced in his direction. "I hope you're right, Brady."

"We'll stick together and watch out for each other, alright?" Brady smiled. "Deal," he continued, extending his hand to Shawn.

Shawn shook his hand. "Deal."

The sound of keys rattling in a lock redirected their gazes to the superintendent, who was hunched forward trying to open a door. A few seconds later, she stood upright again, pushed the door forward, and leaned against the doorpost.

"This way, you two," she told them, straight-faced.

They sauntered past her and stopped midway inside the office. The superintendent closed the door behind them, strolled past them, and walked over to a large office desk with paperwork stacked in neat files. She dropped the file folder she carried on the desk, spun around, and leant against it. With folded arms, she stared at Brady and Shawn, making them uneasy.

"Come over here and have a seat," she commanded, pointing towards the two chairs in front of her.

The boys dragged their feet over to the two chairs and sank into them, keeping their eyes fixed on her.

"You boys don't have to look so tense." The superintendent gave them a tiny smile. "Now, I'm going to tell you what to expect while you are here." She unfolded her arms and rested them on her desk, and then continued. "First thing every morning after breakfast, you will be sent to counselling and anger management sessions. Hopefully, they will help you both to deal with whatever issues you have. After that, high school courses will be provided to help you get your GED to prepare you for college so you can get a job."

Brady raised his hand.

"Yes, Mr. O'Connor, what is it?"

"Hmmm, I already completed my GED, and

recently, too."

"Well, we also have creative courses . . ."

"Do you offer art or painting classes?" he asked with a smile and raised brows.

"Yes, Mr. O'Connor, that is one of the additional main courses offered. The counsellors here said it helps a lot to rehabilitate and reduces hostility among the teens."

"Great, well, sign me up for that, please."

"What about you, Mr. Garcia. Have you also completed your GED?"

"Nope—I mean no. I was too distracted by my domestic problems to focus on schoolwork. Girls were a great distraction," he responded with a smirk, causing Brady to chuckle.

The superintendent reached for the file folder on her desk, pulled out two sheets of paper, then stretched them towards Shawn and Brady.

"Fill these out and make sure to select the right options." After they took the forms from her hands, she continued. "The evenings will be reserved for doing chores, recreation development, and social interaction with other wayward kids like themselves. Oh, here," she added, handing them pens when she realised they were staring at the forms, looking lost.

As soon as Brady and Shawn began to fill out the forms, the superintendent walked around to her desk, picked up her phone receiver, and dialled.

"Can you ask Matron Bull to come to my office now, please?" After a couple of seconds, she added, "Thank you."

She hung the receiver back onto the phone,

pulled out her chair, sank into it, and leaned back. A knock resounded a few minutes later.

"Come in, Matron Bull," the superintendent said and sat up in her chair.

Brady and Shawn lifted their gazes from the forms and turned their heads towards the door. Matron Bull was a middle-aged woman, a bit on the heavy side. She was very muscular and tall. Her steps were heavy and quick. She glanced at the boys once as she walked towards the superintendent's desk. Her fierce expression had them believing she wasn't one to be messed with.

"Matron Bull, this is Mr. O'Connor and Mr. Garcia; they are being placed in your charge. They are going to be with us for the next couple of months until they turn eighteen."

Matron Bull groaned aloud and stared at them in distaste. "What crimes did these two commit?" she scoffed.

"It's all in the file right there," the superintendent informed the matron, pointing to the file folder. "Are you boys finished?" she turned to Brady and Shawn, refocusing their attention back to the forms and from off the matron.

Within another couple of minutes, they stretched the formed towards Matron Bull, who stood closest to them by the desk. She glanced over the forms before she handed them to the superintendent.

"Well, boys, go now with Matron Bull. She will show you where you will be staying for the time you're here."

They nodded and stood to their feet, not too eager to go with Matron Bull. Although the superintendent was firm, she had a warmer personality than what they saw in Matron Bull, who had not even smiled once the whole time she stood in the office.

"Come along, you two," Matron Bull said gruffly as she walked towards the door.

Once they were out of the superintendent's office and walking behind the matron, Shawn nudged Brady to get his attention.

"Remember, you and I have to look out for each other while we're here and ensure neither ends up in the big house."

"The *where?*"

"You forgot so soon. Prison for adults the one the superintendent promises we'll end up if we don't change."

Brady's eyes widened, "Oh yeah, definitely. We certainly won't go there, and we'll be like brothers."

He closed his hand into a fist and pointed to Shawn, who bumped fists with him in agreement and smiled.

As it was already evening when they arrived, the matron showed them first where their sleeping quarters were and then led them to supper before being sent to shower and then to bed.

Their first two weeks there were normal, and it seemed they were adjusting well to the routine of the place. Everyone assumed they were related by how close they stuck to each other. The other boys carefully studied them before going anywhere near them. Shawn and Brady made a pact that they would try not to get into any trouble while at St Peter's, but if anyone bothered either of them, they will deal with them and try not to get caught.

Neither of us is going to the big house after we leave here, they told each other repeatedly. Brady loved his painting classes and grew better each day. Shawn excelled in his courses, and Brady would help him study in the evenings to prepare him to sit the exam near the end of the seven months.

Both boys enjoyed sports, and during the recreational hours, they played basketball a lot. Basketball helped them release their anger and frustration, which they both had bottled up inside. After playing against two other boys as a two-man tag team, they won 3-2, and all now sat resting in the shaded area of the courtyard.

"Here comes Major Stalker," one of the boys groaned when he spotted Matron Bull stomping her way in their direction, causing the others to burst into laughter.

"Why do you all call her that?" Shawn asked with Brady, looking at them with eager curiosity.

"Do you know how sometimes people creep up on you and scare you or how sometimes they end up having things of yours without you knowing how they got it?"

"Yeah," Brady and Shawn nodded.

"Well, she's worse. I suggest that you keep nothing that will get you in trouble in your cells, I should say. She likes going around searching while we're out," the boy cautioned them before Matron Bull approached them.

"You, two, up!" She shouted at the two boys that sat with Brady and Shawn, "Kitchen duty now!" she continued with narrowed eyes.

Reluctantly, they got up and followed behind her.

As Brady and Shawn now sat alone, they turned their gazes to the other boys who were still playing in the courtyard. It amazed them to see so many troubled teens locked up.

"Can you imagine what could have caused them to be in here?" Brady asked Shawn as he pointed over to the said boys playing on the field.

"Well, I know most of them did far worse than you and me. That tall, skinny redhead that just dunked the ball—I heard he killed his parents in their sleep. That short, stocky one suffocated his baby sister with a pillow to get back at his parents. And that thick black guy almost drowned his brother. His father caught him," Shawn reported.

"How do you know all that in the short time we've been here?" Brady stared wide-eyed at him.

Shawn smirked. "Well, I'm quite the talker when I want to be. Although, most times, it's usually negative and harsh words, which would cause my aunt to preach the same Bible verse over and over."

"Reminds me of my grandmother; she always ended our phone calls, letters, or cards with a Bible verse," Brady shared with a chuckle. "What verse did your aunt always give you?"

"Oh man, how could I forget that? I have heard it so often. Wait a minute . . . I think it's coming back," he laughed. *'He who guards his mouth preserves his life, but he who opens wide his lips shall have destruction. Proverbs 13:3.'*"

"I think I got that one from Gram, too,"

Brady laughed. "Hey, why do you and your friend choose to hang out in that lonely, unpleasant place where we met?"

"Carlos and I chose that place because it's the farthest place we could find to escape our homes. We both had drunken, abusive fathers. I know what we were doing out there was not good. I think we only resorted to robbery because our mums were struggling to make ends meet without our dad's support."

"You said both had. Does that mean Carlos's dad is also dead?"

"Yeah, he died," Shawn chuckled. And to think it's because he didn't take heed to that verse Aunt Marie always tells me. One of his friends stabbed him because of something he had said. I don't even know what it was he had said either."

Brady shared with Shawn the full story of losing John and the traumatic effects it had on him, leading to his drug addiction, as well as the real reason he ended up in Miami with his dad. He felt good to have a friend again, almost like a brother to talk to.

CHAPTER 18- SURVIVAL

Life at St. Peter's was relatively normal with the exception of the boys who thought they should be bullies to everyone else, seeing them on a thin line of heading straight to the big house upon reaching eighteen.

Each time these bullies found Brady or Shawn alone, they would pound on them, showing their strength. Both boys took their beatings willingly without giving in to the bullies' demands. This made them regular targets for getting kicked and punched around.

Each time they were abused, Matron Bull asked them to name their assailants, but they would not give any names, making everyone think they were scared, including the bullies. This act continued for the first three months.

Brady, Shawn, and Ricky—a friend of theirs, who was two inches shorter than them and of

Asian and black descent—sat out in the courtyard one afternoon and watched as two bullies went into the courtyard's bathroom.

"Remember the signal," Shawn told Ricky as he and Brady followed the bullies towards the bathroom.

Upon entering, they walked straight towards the bullies, who stood facing the urinals, grabbed their heads, and slammed them against the walls. The sudden impact of the bullies' heads colliding with the wall caused them to pass out instantly.

Brady and Shawn hastily wiped the traces of blood from the wall. They stepped over the unconscious bodies and darted from the bathroom to reoccupy their seats next to Ricky, just in time to see Matron Bull walking towards them.

"Get to the cafeteria now for dinner!" she ordered.

Twenty minutes later, two bullies busted through the cafeteria doors, furious. Everyone's gaze turned to them. They glared around at all the boys while blood dripped down their busted faces, hoping to see guilt written on the culprits.

Matron Bull knew they were not saints. She didn't give them time to explain whether their bruises resulted from their mischief. She urgently escorted them from the room and isolated them for two weeks after seeing the nurse.

The whole dinner hall fell silent while Matron Bull reprimanded and escorted the boys from the cafeteria, much to their victims' delight. Both Brady and Shawn chuckled to themselves.

The disciplinary action Matron Bull enforced did not affect the continuous harassment that the remaining eight bullies inflicted on others. Brady and Shawn were fighting very hard to hold in their anger and frustration until they could not any longer.

"Brady, we can't continue to let them beat us up like this. I don't know how much more my ribs can take," Shawn shared with his friend as they ate their meal one evening.

"I know," Brady whispered. "I have a plan that will keep them from hurting us or anyone else for the remainder of our time here at St. Peter's."

"Well, what is it?" Shawn asked, eager to know.

"I will tell you about it tomorrow during yard duty, where it's safe," he shared while his eyes scanned around for itchy ears.

The bullies had enforced their own rules, where during recreational hours, they must always use the courtyard first. So, whenever Brady, Shawn, or any other of the juveniles were out on the court playing, they would have to run off the courts when the bully team arrived. This was where they'd pounce on many because they all had some level of rebellion and often resisted.

Today, being officially four months since Brady and Shawn came to St. Peter's, was the day they aimed to execute their plan against the bullies. When the bullies came and demanded the courts, not one of the boys made a fuss. All of them walked off like defeated foes, causing the bullies to laugh hard at them. They all sat begrudgingly on the sidelines, watching the bullies as they played out their full match. No one fussed, which gave the bullies an uneasy feeling.

After they concluded their match and walked off the court, they kept their eyes fixed on the boys as they gave them access back to the court. This made some of the younger boys smile and rush back onto the courtyard while a large group got up with screwed faces, muttering curses under their breaths, walking away toward the dining hall. Only a few boys remained sitting on the sidelines with Brady and Shawn. They conversed with each other, pretending not to notice the bullies at all.

The bullies took that as a sign that all was well, and most followed the large crowd to the dinner hall, leaving two who went to the restroom. They still had an hour before dinner was served, which meant Matron Bull would not be coming around to chase them off to dinner. Because the dining hall had now become a hangout spot for those who were uninterested in playing sports when it was way too hot or even too cold, it made the boy's plan safe.

Back in the courtyard, while the younger ones entertain themselves on the court, Brady, Shawn, and Ricky stepped into action.

"You all remember the plan, right?" Brady asked the boys, who were seated with them on the sidelines.

The boys nodded.

Feeling pleased, Brady, Shawn, and Ricky got up and walked towards the bathroom. The two bullies were already inside two of the toilet cubicles when Brady and Shawn stepped inside.

They smiled at each other as they took their places inside an empty cubicle next to the ones the bullies occupied.

Ricky, who remained outside the bathroom door, locked it and waited. Brady and Shawn flushed the toilet as if they had used it, stepped out, and waited by the faucets washing their hands. The two bullies stepped out of the cubicles.

They glanced at each other with menacing smiles, seeing two other juveniles standing by the sink. They walked over to the faucets and shoved Brady and Shawn aside, turned the tap on, and proceeded to wash their hands. Brady and Shawn regained their balance, and instead of running from the bathroom as the bullies expected, they stood and glared at them hard.

The bullies' eyes turned to face Brady and Shawn with curiosity. They had never seen such intense stares from any of the other boys who had ever resisted them.

"You think you can challenge us and win?" the redhead of the two snickered.

"Well, there are two of you and two of us, so it will be a fair fight," Shawn said and glanced at Brady, who only smiled.

The other bully, who had dark hair scrutinised Brady as they stood there and stepped in front of him. "I don't like you," he emphasised with a gruff voice. "I never liked you from the day you showed up here with your pretty boy look. I am going to mess that face up so no woman will bear to look at you to even go out on a date with you."

Brady arched a brow at him and kept

smiling, contributing to the bully's annoyance.

"You know, you and your friend are going to be badly beaten here today, right?" he spat out at Brady.

Brady's smile faded. "So, you say, but know that today is the last day you will ever lay hands on my brother or me."

That was the signal Shawn needed, and without warning, he slammed his fist into the red-haired bully's face, facing him. As he staggered, Shawn pounded sharp, continuous blows into his ribs, left and right. Brady took quick action threw solid punches at his opponent's face and chest, not giving him a chance to fire back.

The force and swiftness of the blows caused both bullies to stagger and fall. But just as quickly as they fell, they were back on their feet, ready to return punches.

Brady and Shawn were ready and gave them every bit of what they had held back from months of enduring all their assaults. Both had forgotten they did not want to resort back to the rage, which landed them at St. Peter's. They gave the boys everything they had and beat them senseless, unrelenting by the couple punches or kicks they received themselves.

After ten minutes or so, Ricky stuck his head inside and alerted them. "Major stalker is coming!" he shouted almost in a panic.

"Calm down! Have you forgotten the boys are outside to keep her distracted? Just give us the duct tapes and keep a lookout and say when she's two steps from the door, alright," Shawn ordered him.

"Okay! Okay!" Ricky replied, handing them the tapes and stepping back outside.

The bullies, who were too weak to fight back at this point, opened their eyes wide and tried to muster the strength to cry out. Brady and Shawn taped their mouths shut, not giving them a chance. They duct-taped the bullies' hands in front of them and quickly led them back into the toilet cubicles.

They propped them on top of the flush bowl to sit, just as Ricky rushed in, alerting them that Matron Bull was two steps away. As they stood inside the cubicles in front of the boys and waited, they held onto the bully's necks with one hand. The other hand formed a fist, aimed at their faces, warning them to be still.

Ricky entered a cubicle. All three boys stood still and waited.

Walking into a boys' bathroom was no strange thing for Matron Bull, who has seen her share of craziness at St. Peter's. It kept her on her toes. As she walked along each cubicle, she bent down to see how many were occupied. Standing back upright, she spoke. "Was there a fight in here just now? Look at this place. I don't know how many times we've replaced these toilet paper holders and even the mirrors," she lamented.

As she inspected the place, Ricky stepped out as if he had just finished using the toilet and went to wash his hands.

"What happened in here, Ricky?" she asked with a no-nonsense look on her face.

"Well, there was a fight, Matron Bull. I heard it while I walked down here. But by the time I got to the door, two boys almost knocked me over by the speed at which they rushed out, and then I saw the other hop past me," he told her very convincingly.

She listened with folded arms, although suspicious of his story. "And those two in there, who sound like they have diarrhoea?" she arched her brow, awaiting his response.

Turning his nose up, Ricky added, "I came in here and heard them, too, and thought I ought to hurry before the stink came," he continued. "Can I go now?" he asked her, quite eager to leave.

"Go ahead," she motioned with a wave of her hand, and he rushed out, leaving her facing the two cubicles now. "All right, it's just you two and myself here, and I want your names right NOW."

"Brady."

"And Shawn."

"Ahhh . . . you two! I wonder if there is more to it than what Ricky told me. Anyways, I want you two out of here in the next ten minutes, so you better hold in some of what you're trying so hard to squeeze out." With that said, she walked out.

Whew, both boys let out a sigh of relief and cautiously stepped out of the stalls with their victims.

"Now what?" Shawn asked Brady, who was more into action than talking. "We can't leave them here now. She'll know it was us."

Brady smiled, "Don't worry; we won't get caught. Remember our motto. We'll leave them in the cherry bushes behind the restroom. Let's strip them first, so they will be preoccupied while we finish up with you know what," he laughed.

"Great idea, Brady," Shawn replied, laughing back.

Brady peeped outside. After getting a safe signal from the few boys who were still playing on the courts, they stripped the boys that were unconscious from being punched and took them under the cherry bushes before hiding their clothes.

Brady, Shawn, and the remaining boys on the court rushed off to the dining hall and joined the others. As soon as the last boy entered the dining hall, they all stood by the door, laughing as if enjoying a joke they shared from on the courts. One of them quietly bolted the locks on the door.

Still, with thirty minutes until dinner, they, along with the others who had entered the dining hall earlier, approached the bullies' table. One by one, they struck them. Although the bullies fought hard—bruising many—the boys did not relent. They soon had all the bullies on the ground, groaning in pain from kicks, punches, and even bites from the younger juveniles, who didn't have enough strength to throw an effective punch or kick.

"We only have about fifteen minutes before Major Stalker arrives!" Brady yelled as he bent down and held onto one of the bully's arms. Another boy assisted him.

"C'mon, guys, hurry," Shawn said, grabbing hold of another bully under his arm and headed towards the door.

"Open the doors, Mark!" Brady shouted at the tall boy near the door.

Brady, Shawn, and a couple of other boys

hurried, dragging the bullies out of the dinner hall. They locked them in a nearby room and rushed back into the dining hall.

Although they all had sustained blows from the bullies, they took their usual places and tried to suppress their aching.

When dinner was served, Matron Bull began to suspect foul play and noticed that some of the boys were missing. She noticed that even though everyone was still in their normal mood, they looked a bit antsy. She barely stifled laughter when the door burst open: two naked boys rushed in, covering their genitals. Eight more followed closely behind them, groaning in pain.

"Well, this has been quite a day. But I suspect that you boys are the cause of all the mischief that has been happening all these months and are now paying for it. *What*! You expected me to sympathise with you," she mocked and jeered them, causing the other boys to snicker quietly. "I'm sorry to add further pain to your already injured pride and body parts. But you boys will be confined to solitary after you all see the nurse and get cleaned up. There will be no meals for you tonight either," she concluded just before calling another matron to escort them to the infirmary. Then she let out the laughter that she could no longer contain.

"Boys," she began quite calmly. "I don't believe in violence, but I am proud that you have for once fought back and did it without dangerous weapons. Every once in a while, it's good to stand up for yourself to keep people from continually trampling you. Brady and Shawn, I know you two are the brains behind this act today. However, I will let this one slide, but I want no repeat of this from anyone. Do I make myself clear?"

"Yes, Major Stalk—Matron Bull," they all shouted, almost in fright, causing her to laugh.

"It's okay, boys. I knew your nickname for me all along. Remember, a stalker knows everything," she teased, causing everyone to laugh, then relaxed.

Since that day, everything got better for all the boys; even the bullies started to change. They realised that they were too young to end up in prison for a long time or even worse—forever.

CHAPTER 19- MAKING AMENDS

At the end of the seven months, Brady, Shawn, and all the other boys, who had also reached the age of eighteen now, stood at the entrance once again, facing Superintendent Watkins. She had another speech for them again, but this time, she was a bit more warm and sincere.

"Boys, I hope that being inside this facility has taught you something about the importance of being responsible. That when you are careless and irresponsible, you can find yourselves in places that can be harsh and tough, where you are unable to see or be around loved ones. I sincerely pray that the good Lord will guide you as you continue to grow and experience life with its ups and downs. And give you the strength and courage to stand strong to face it, *without* resorting to an evil that can land you in the big house, which is far worse than here. Good luck, and may God go with you all." With that said, she shook their hands and gave them a bright smile.

Superintendent Watkins stood and watched while they all got on the bus. She gave the driver a list and instructed him as to where each boy was to be dropped off and what officer would receive them at their designated stop.

Since they were on their way home, they were allowed to sit anywhere they wish but still had to maintain disciplined, as not to cause chaos for the driver, who had to focus on his driving and also keep an eye on them. The bus was quite secure for both the driver and the boys. It had a built-in security bar, which separated the driver from them, and a security lock on the door, which could only be opened by the driver.

Shawn and Brady smiled all the way back to Miami and enjoyed the time they had with their other friends, who were also going home. Ricky was also in the lot but would get off before them. As he came close to his stop, he turned to Shawn and Brady and grabbed hold of each of their hand.

"You guys helped me to stand up to those bullies at St. Peter's. The things I did that brought me there was just my way of defending myself. I never knew how to defend myself until you guys had taught me, so thank you both. I always hated knives and other weapons. Hey! I have an idea. How about we all meet in five years at my family's farm and see where we are in life? If, however, by some predicament, it doesn't happen for all of us to show up, we can go to Brady's next. What do you say, guys?" he said, eyes sparkling. His smile broadened.

"Sounds great to me," Shawn piped in.

"Yeah, for me, too," Brady added. "But let's meet out at my grandmother's, okay? It's the best place I can think of to find creative inspiration to paint. You guys will love it there, too."

For Ricky, it was bittersweet when the bus came to a halt. He heard his name called, along with a few others. He hugged his good friends and ran off the bus. The routine became the same for Brady and Shawn, with the rest of their friends for the remainder of the journey.

"Shawn," Brady said, facing him. "I think my dad is going to send me back to my Mum."

"Why? Would he still be upset with you after so long?"

"I don't know if he'll still be upset, but I don't think he'll want me around after what transpired between us. That is not what bothers me, though. It is the thought of having to face whatever is to come without my closest friend. You're my brother, Shawn."

"Likewise, Brady, you're my best friend and brother. And if you're going to leave Miami, I will truly miss you."

Both sat silently as the bus pulled up at the station.

"Brady O'Connor, Shawn Garcia!" the driver called when he opened the door, waiting for them to step from the bus. Neither moved until their names were called again, and one of the other boys nudged them.

As they walked into the station, they tried to suppress the melancholy that overwhelmed them. The officer led them to the front desk to hand them over to the inspector.

Shaw's aunt was already there, seated and waiting. When she saw him, she sprung to her feet and rushed towards them.

"Hold on, ma'am," the officer stretched out his hand towards her. "We have to complete the paperwork here first before we hand him over to you. Just go back and have a seat. You'll be able to take him home in a few minutes," the officer advised her after she almost knocked him over by her anxiety.

She nodded and scrambled back to where she previously sat. She watched as the inspector did his checks and then let both Brady and Shawn sign some paperwork.

"Well," he said, staring at them both, "I hope you boys don't hate me for sending you to Judge Ryan. I just hate to see young people destroy their lives before they get a chance to make something useful of it."

They both smiled.

"We don't hate you, Sir," Brady spoke on their behalf. "If it wasn't for you, we wouldn't have become brothers," he added as he placed his hand on Shawn's shoulder, who also smiled in agreement.

"Well, I'm so pleased that things turned out good in both your favours. I hope you will now try and keep out of further trouble. You're now free to go," he concluded.

When Marie heard the inspector speak those words, she jumped to her feet and ran over to the boys. Tears filled her eyes, "Shawn!" she said, causing him and Brady to spin around. Marie pulled him into a tight embrace, and Shawn wrapped his arms around her feeling grateful.

"I'm sorry that I didn't come to see you, Shawn," she told him after she released him from her embrace. "They said visitors weren't allowed," she lamented.

"I know, Aunt Marie; they told us the first week we were there. I think it was their strategy to prevent us from returning. It's probably what caused Brady and me to bond. Aunt Marie, you remember Brady? We started as enemies but returned as brothers," he chuckled. "I told him that he can come to visit us anytime he wishes. I hope you don't mind." Shawn told her as he introduced her to Brady.

Marie smiled and shook Brady's hand. "Nice to meet you, Brady, and you're welcome to visit us anytime. I think it would be great for Shawn, too, since he doesn't have many good friends around him."

"Nice to meet you, too, Marie. You'll probably see more of me than you would like," he smiled.

"Oh! Aunt Marie, I have a surprise," Shawn interjected, excited. He withdrew an envelope from his bag, gave it to her, and watched her expression.

"This is wonderful, Shawn. This will now help you get a good job, or even get into college if you so desire," she beamed.

Brady watched as Shawn shared his test scores with his aunt and could not help but smile, feeling happy for them both. But, then, his face grew sad at the thought that they had already been at the station for almost twenty minutes, and no one had yet shown up to pick him up.

"Marie, have you seen my dad or my stepmum?" he asked as he scanned the place for signs of them.

"No, I haven't seen anyone, and I have been waiting here for quite some time. I'm sorry, dear, maybe they are stuck in traffic," she told him, trying to remove the disappointment on his face.

"It's all right," he smiled to hide the look of hurt.

Within a few minutes, they heard a car screech to a halt in front of the station and saw Denise rushing inside the station.

"Hello," she said to everyone as she approached Brady, Shawn, and Marie. "That old car broke down on the freeway, and it took me twenty minutes to get help." She gave Brady a tight hug and kissed his cheek, making him smile, knowing that he was not abandoned.

"Why didn't Dad pick me up, Denise?" he asked after she released him from her hug.

Uncertain of how to answer without making him feel bad, she smiled while she caressed his cheek. "Brady, you know your dad is a stubborn, hard-headed man. He has forgiven you but wasn't ready to face you, or, as he said, 'not out here.' He said when you get home, you and he will talk."

Brady introduced Denise to Shawn, and Marie then turned to Shawn. "Well, whatever the outcome, I'll come to see you before I leave." The two men embraced, hoping it wasn't the last time they would see each other for a while. They said their goodbyes.

Brady didn't say much during the drive back to his dad's house. He appreciated Denise for how much she cared for him, even with being his step-mum, but he couldn't believe that after all that time, his dad was still not totally over it. *Hasn't he ever made a mistake, for goodness sake?* Brady thought to himself as he stared out the window.

"Cheer up, Brady. I can see you sulking over there," Denise said as she drove, glancing over at him occasionally.

"I'm fine, Denise, *honestly,*" he replied, not taking his eyes from the window.

When they got home, Frank was nowhere to be seen. This was why he preferred his mother to his father. She was always so quick to forgive and never held a grudge. Even while his parents were married, his dad was the same way, always held on to bitterness. It was part of the reason they couldn't stay together. Only Denise seemed to be able to deal with his temperamental mood changes, which seemed to be the reason their marriage has lasted as long as it has.

Denise made him some lunch, and afterwards, Brady took a nap and slept until dinnertime. Denise woke him. When he walked out into the dining room to the dinner table, his dad was already seated and with a surprisingly pleasant look on his face.

Brady took his place at the table and fixed his eyes on his dad while they waited for Denise to finish placing the final part of the meal on the table.

The minute Frank took notice of Brady staring at him, he spoke. "Brady," he sighed. "I'm sorry I was so harsh on you that night when I realised you smoked marijuana at the party. I dealt with the situation badly, and I should have trusted you to know your limits and be responsible after all the progress you had made. After losing one son, I feared the worst happening to you, and I couldn't risk losing you, too. Can you blame me? You're all I have left." Tears welled up in his eyes. "I don't think you even know how much I love you, Brady. You remind me so much of myself, and I'm sorry I hurt your feelings."

Brady was taken aback, seeing his dad at the point of tears and now expressing how much he loved him. He reached across the table, taking hold of his father's hand. He squeezed it and smiled.

"I love you, too, Dad. I, too, am sorry. I should have tried to control my temper and listened to you."

By this time, Denise had joined them at the table and sat watching the two men making amends. She smiled. She had spoken to Frank, making him realise that he was too hard on Brady, who had been working hard to straighten his life out and only needed his father's guidance, not his wrath. It reminded Frank how much he himself had sought his own father's approval when he was young, and it made him remorseful.

"All right, you two; let's eat now, and you can finish your conversation later," she put in, causing both to smile.

Later that night, Brady and Frank sat out on the verandah and enjoyed the cool night air. Frank drank a cold beer while Brady had some cranberry juice.

"Dad, I miss Mum, and I know she must be

lonely, too," Brady spoke, breaking the silence.

"Yes, she does; she often calls and asks about you. I could hear it in her voice that she does. Maybe it's time you go back home since you're doing well now. I will miss you, but I think she needs you more. You can always come back to visit whenever you wish."

"I think you're right, Dad, but I want to visit my friend before I go back. So, I will stay for the next two weeks then return home, alright?"

"Okay, Son, as you wish."

For the next two weeks, Brady's relationship with his dad went back to normal, and he continued to help with the store. Later, in the evenings, he would head over to Shawn's, where he spent most of the night. Shawn even took him to the nursing home to visit and meet his mother, who was always happy whenever Shawn arrived.

Shawn came to the airport to see him off, along with Frank and Denise. This was a period in Brady's life when he was happy again, but now he was leaving the people he had come to find joy around. Knowing it was not forever, his heart felt peace. He was looking forward to seeing his mum again, and with that in his thoughts, he hugged everyone and said his goodbyes.

CHAPTER 20- BREAKING BAD HABITS FOR GOOD

"Mum!"

Claudette's face radiated at the sound of Brady's voice as he stepped through the terminal's exit. She dashed towards him.

Brady hastened his steps to meet her halfway.

Claudette giggled in delight when Brady scooped her up in his arms upon contact. Joy permeated her when Brady pressed wet kisses against her cheeks, and she saw the broad smile on his face. She closed her eyes and thanked God for His guiding hand over Brady.

"I have missed you, Brady," she said, her feet back on the ground.

"I've missed you, too, Mum—I have so much to tell you!"

Claudette looped her arm through Brady's, "Let's get home, and you can tell me all about it."

"Okay, Mum."

Within three weeks of being home, Brady got a job at an advertising company with his artistic skills and high test scores. He loved that while creating great ad images, he was also gaining experience, which would provide him greater opportunities in marketing. Life for him now seemed to be on track, and he began to enjoy his life.

Shawn, on the other hand, found it a little harder to get a job. Most people could not see past the violent threats he used to inflict upon everyone.

"Aunt Marie," Shawn sighed while they sat down to dinner one evening. "How will I be able to provide for you and mum?" he lamented.

"What do you mean, Shawn? Have you forgotten I have a job, and your mother's life insurance is taking care of her at the nursing home?" Marie responded, a bit confused.

"I know that, Aunt Marie, but your job at the hair salon can do only so much, and besides, I'm eighteen now, and I want to take my responsibility as the man of the house. I just can't let you shoulder the responsibilities alone. Everywhere I apply has rejected me. No one wants to believe that I have changed. How do you stand strong when everything seems to be against you?"

Marie saw the strain on him, she reached across the table, and squeezed his hand. "I trust in the Lord," she started. "And it's something you will need to start doing more than ever now." She sighed and continued. "People will need time to trust that the words you now declare about yourself are true—it's our actions that allow others to start believing in us.

"Until that happens, you will have to stand strong in the face of whatever oppositions or rejections that comes your way. I know it may seem strange for you to understand my level of trust in God, Shawn, because sometimes you don't see anything happen when I pray. But God always knows when to best answer our prayers and bring an answer.

"Sometimes it's hard to wait, especially when it looks like we are backed against the wall, but even then, He's still at work. Shawn, for the sake of your mum, have a little faith in God and do not give up. He will turn up for you. The devil just likes to rub our past in our faces to make us quit when he sees that we are near the things we ask God for. God is not a quitter.

"If he was, we wouldn't have salvation today. For us, who choose to trust and surrender our will to Him, and receive His Holy Spirit, and have His spirit living in us, transforming us, we cannot allow the devil to deceive us into thinking we are quitters. This is why you see me praying even when I feel worn out sometimes, and whenever I come close to doing that, the Lord always gives me the same Scripture to know that He's there."

"What Scripture?"

"Isaiah 43:1-5; it says, *'Fear not for I have redeemed you, I have called you by your name; thou art mine. When you pass through the waters; and through the rivers, they shall not overflow thee: when you walk through the fire, you shall not be burnt; neither shall the flame kindle upon you. For I am the Lord thy God, the Holy One of Israel, thy Saviour: I gave up Egypt for thy ransom, Ethiopia and Seba for thee. Since you are precious in my sight, you have been honourable, and I have loved thee: therefore will I give men for thee and people for your life. Fear not for I am with you.'"*

"I like that verse, Aunt Marie—it's very encouraging. I won't give up," Shawn said with optimism.

The next couple of weeks still saw no light at the end of the tunnel for Shawn. His thoughts were scattered as he walked along an abandoned train track one afternoon. Soon, he found a quiet spot and sat down.

His head pounded as his mind sieve through all the different options he could think of to earn some money—that is, without getting himself into trouble. He felt the desperation of not knowing where to turn, and he cried out.

"Heavenly Father, if You are as real as my aunt believes You are, please help me. Show up for me and come to my rescue. Help me see You the way she sees You and trusts in You. Help me to not resort back to the way I was, for Mum and Aunt Marie's sake. Show me what my purpose on earth is so that I can see myself more than how everyone sees me—this destructive person who doesn't deserve a second chance. I now see the wisdom in the verses my aunt used to tell me. I wished I had listened when she tried to steer me in the right direction." He took a deep breath and continued. *"I repent for every word I have spoken in the past to and of anyone in a hurtful way. Father, Aunt Marie had always said, You use*

both the good and bad for Your purpose. So let not the bad I have done in the past rob me of the good You can use me to do for Your purpose. Whatever Your will for me is, Father, I hand my life over into Your hands and ask for Your mercy. I know that if no one else can see any good in me, You can, by how my aunt talks about You. All I ask, Father, is that you help me provide for my family in Jesus's name. Amen."

Shawn dropped his head into his hands and wept in despair.

Ten minutes passed. A loud clanking forced Shawn to lift his head and begin glancing around. He spotted an old man—about sixty and of a medium build—a couple of paces away, struggling to pull some steel pipes over the tracks. Shawn jumped to his feet and ran towards the man, then reached for the pipes that were slipping from the man's hold.

"Let me help you with those, Sir."

The old man let out a deep breath, glanced up at Shawn, and smiled. "Oh, thank you so much, young man." He released the remaining pipes to Shawn.

"Where are you taking these, Sir?"

"I'm heading over to my house on Miracle Mile."

"Miracle Mile?" Shawn's brows furrowed in surprise. "That is quite a distance for a man of your age to be carrying such heavy pipes by yourself."

"Yes, my boy, young people these days aren't quite as helpful to older folks like myself. The rule to respect your elders, which I grew up on, is gone with the wind with this generation."

Shawn adjusted the pipes in his hands and followed the old man. When they arrived at his house, Shawn smiled, admiring the nice house the man owned.

"Will you come inside and have a drink to refresh yourself before you go?"

"Thank you, Sir."

"What were you doing out on those tracks alone, young man? You looked quite distraught." The old man stretched a glass of cranberry juice to Shawn, then sat down across from him and crossed his legs.

Shawn related his story, and the man smiled. "You know, it seemed I was meant to meet you today. You see, I lost my only son and my wife recently in a car accident: he was taking her home from church. I had spoken to the Lord about sending me a strong young man to help me around here, and it seems you're his choice."

"I'm sorry about your loss, Sir," Shawn offered as he listened attentively. "But what do you mean?"

"I could have hired someone to carry the pipes for me today, but the Lord told me to walk. Someone will show up, He said. You're the one who did," the man chuckled. "What's your name, young man?"

"Shawn . . . Shawn Garcia, Sir."

"Call me Mr. Jones. Would you like a job, Shawn? I raise cattle and sell the meat to restaurants and food stores. I have three young men working with me now, but two are going off to college in a few weeks."

A big smile spread across Shawn's face. He could not believe God had shown up so soon for him. It made him think about his poor aunt, whom he had seen praying to God many times and oftentimes waited for months—sometimes longer—before answers came, sometimes even getting a little discouraged.

"Well . . ." Mr. Jones said, breaking his happy thought.

"Yes! Mr. Jones, I want the job."

"It is hard work, you know. Think you are up for it?"

"Yes, Sir, I can manage and will do my best." Shawn's heart raced with excitement. "Thank you for giving me a chance."

Mr. Jones laughed and then stood to his feet. "Excuse me for a bit," he said before leaving the room. When he returned and sat back down across from Shawn, he stretched his hand towards Shawn. "Here, take this."

"What is this for, Sir?" Shawn stared in confusion. "Is it for carrying those pipes?—I didn't do it for money. It was just the right thing to do," he rambled on, not making an effort to take it from Mr. Jones' hand.

"It's all right, Shawn." Mr. Jones chuckled. "I know you didn't, and this isn't for that either. I just felt in my spirit to do so, so take it." He stretched the money towards Shawn again and smiled even more when Shawn took it from his hands. "Shawn, I know you can handle the job," Mr. Jones added with full confidence.

"Thank you, Mr. Jones," Shawn beamed, full of gratitude.

"Can you show up the day after tomorrow at 8:00 a.m. so the young men can start showing you the routine of the farm?"

"I certainly can!"

"Wonderful. Now, try to get on home safe."

"Okay, Mr. Jones will do, and thank you again. Good evening."

As Shawn walked along the not-so-busy street, he could not believe his good fortune. "My word, one hundred dollars this man gives me, and I haven't started working yet. I wonder what my salary will be if he can afford to give me this much, just because he felt to do so." Shawn smiled to himself, "Thank you, Lord, for showing me that you are real and that You come to our aid when we call upon You."

****

"Aunt Marie! Aunt Marie!" Shawn yelled through the house, unable to contain his excitement.

Marie rushed from her bedroom with fear in her eyes.

"What's wrong?"

Shawn hunched forward, resting his hands on his knees, and tried to catch his breath.

"Come," Marie said, gently rubbing his back, "you go sit down in the living room; I'll get you some water, and you can tell me all about it, okay?"

Shawn nodded while trying to steady his breath, then he headed towards the living room and slumped into the sofa.

"Here you go, drink." Marie handed him the glass of water and sat down next to him.

Shawn gulped the water down before taking a breath, and then he relayed his story.

"Wow, Shawn!" Marie's eyes widened in excitement. "That's great news. You see, my dear; God is always listening to us when we call upon Him, and as I said before, He knows when to answer our prayers." She pressed a light kiss on his cheek. "Tonight, I'm going to make you a special dinner."

Shawn reached for Marie's hand and placed the money in it. "This is for you, Aunt Marie."

Marie stared down at rolls of twenty-dollar bills in her hand, and a tear fell. She smiled and stretched her hand towards him. "No Shawn, God gave you that money . . ."

"And now I'm giving it to you. I have a job now, remember?" he smiled, closing her fingers over it, and she smiled.

****

Since Brady left Miami, he and Shawn spoke on the telephone at least once a week. Shawn had updated Brady of his new job and his newfound faith in Christ. Now a year had passed, and today, when Brady called Shawn, he knew something was wrong.

"Hey, Shawn, you don't sound so good. What's wrong?" he asked when Shawn picked up the receiver.

"It's Mr. Jones; his health has declined a lot over this past year."

"I'm sorry, Shawn, but I know he's glad to have you there. I think that's why he taught you everything about his business and put you in charge."

"Yeah, it's just hard to sit and watch him suffer so much. He's been like a father to me in so many ways, Brady," Shawn choked on the words. "Aunt Marie comes over to the house after work and helps me take care of him when I have to go do the accounts."

"I'm glad you took my advice and got Mr. Jones to hire a few more hands to help you before it got this bad, now that business is doing so well. How is your mum doing now? Last time you said she was speaking a little."

"She's doing great," he said, sounding a bit more cheerful. "How is your mum?"

"She's great as usual—still worries about me like I'm her baby," he chuckled, "but that's mum. Remember when I told you that ever since I came home, she sneaks by my door to check up on me?"

"Yeah."

"Well, now she only does it on Saturdays, after I return home from going out with my work colleagues."

Shawn chuckled, "Maybe she still fears you're doing drugs again, Brady."

"I think she does. I have to admit, though, Shawn, every now and then, I smoke a little weed after I get home from the parties."

"Are you crazy? Why would you even want to smoke that after what happened between you and your dad?"

"Not crazy, Shawn. It just helps me to relax, and I always go up on the roof and smoke it before I go to bed."

"Well, just be careful, okay? I don't want to hear anything bad happen to you."

"I will; I hope Mr. Jones recovers, too. Talk to you later."

"You too, Brady."

Since Shawn spoke to Brady about him smoking marijuana, Brady became extra careful over the next couple of weeks. However, after returning home one Saturday night from his friends' hangout spot, he felt a bit more worn out than usual. He didn't have the energy to climb the steps to the roof to smoke his leftover weed from the previous week. Since it was just a small piece, he decided to smoke it right there in his room. After smoking the joint, he instantly fell asleep.

Claudette had a bad feeling as she walked towards Brady's room. Fear gripped her the minute she stood in front of his door—she smelled smoke. Her heart pounded and panicked set in. She grabbed the doorknob, hoping Brady had listened to her about not bolting his room door at night.

A sigh of relief escaped her lips as she pushed the door open. She gasped in terror; flames had already engulfed half of Brady's room. Claudette scampered over to Brady's bed and shook him hard.

"Brady, wake up!" she shouted. He did not budge.

Claudette crouched by his bed and wrapped his arms around her neck, then braced him against her back, dragging his deadweight out of the room. The fire had begun to spread throughout the house as she made her way through the passageway towards the front door.

"Brady! Wake up!" she screamed, jerking him against her, her heart throbbing fast.

Claudette felt the heat tailing her as she inched closer and closer to the front door. She shifted Brady against her shoulder and picked up her pace, glancing back every few steps.

"Almost there, Brady," she let out between short breaths.

A couple of steps away from the door, Claudette yelped in pain when her ankle twisted in the rectangular carpet, which stretched throughout the entire corridor towards the front door. She screamed as her ankle gave way, and she went down, causing Brady to slide down her back.

A tear fell from Claudette's eyes, and she let out a deep breath. *"Lord, Jesus, help me get Brady out of this house. If anyone should die today, let it be me; I could not bear surviving the death of my two sons. I know you have a plan for Brady; help him find his way."*

With determination, Claudette pushed herself up on her feet and repositioned Brady's body against her back. The fire was closing in on her and Brady as she closed the gap between them and the front door. With a firm grip on Brady, she yanked back the locks on the door, flung the door open, and dragged them both out, wincing in pain on her twisted ankle.

Beads of sweat dripped down Brady's face and neck, and he groaned against Claudette's neck. He felt a burning sensation all over his back and thought he must be dreaming until he felt its sting. His eyes flew open, and panic set in when he saw the fire bursting through the front door behind them.

"Fi—fire!" he panicked, trying to gain his balance, pulling his hands from his mother's neck. In his frenzy, he tripped, pulling his mum down with him, and they both tumbled down the seven steps. Their bodies banged hard against the sharp edges until they both lay unconscious at the foot of the steps.

****

"Sir, can you hear me?" a deep masculine voice drummed into Brady's head.

Brady squeezed his eyes shut, trying to drum out the massive headache he felt. His body felt like he had been a victim of a gang beat down. His eyes fluttered open to see a firefighter staring down at him.

"What happened?" He heaved as he tried to sit up and groaned in anguish.

"Hold on, Sir," you have minor burns to your back. You have to stay still."

"Burns . . . from what?" he uttered with a dry, hoarse voice.

The man's eyes glanced behind him, and Brady's eyes followed his.

Ah, yes, now it all was coming back—the fire and the fall. His heart pounded hard, and his breathing intensified. "Where is my mother?"

"They just put her in the ambulance; she has no burns, but she's badly injured. Did you both fall down these steps?"

"Yes." Tears filled his eyes, "Can you take me to her, please?" he croaked.

The firefighter nodded and motioned to two paramedics to come over. "Put him with his mum."

Inside the ambulance on the way to the hospital, Brady lay on his stomach while the paramedic cut opened the back of his shirt and applied a cool compress to ease his burn. His eyes were fixed on his mum, whose eyes had remained shut the whole time. She looked so at peace, even with the oxygen mask she wore.

"Sir," the paramedic said, causing Brady to

shift his gaze. "Take these—they are for the pain."

The young man gave him a polite smile and placed the two pills into his hands and a small cup of water. Brady quickly swallowed the pills and downed them with the water, after which the paramedic sat down and let him relax. Brady's eyes went back to his mum, and he reached for her hand and squeezed gently.

"Mum, wake up."

She groaned in pain before her eyes fluttered opened and stared up at him. Claudette took two deep breathes before she spoke. "You're okay." She smiled then began to cough violently, which manifested fright on Brady's face.

"Mum, I can't lose you, too. I will not make it if you die. You are always where I find the strength to get through each day," he sobbed aloud.

"Brady," she said barely above a whisper, "you must live for my sake if I don't make it. Promise me that you won't go back to doing those things again," she pleaded, staring at him with so much love and concern still in her eyes.

"You won't—you can't die, Mum," he continued refusing to accept that she could die.

Choking on her breath, she spoke again, "Please, Son, promise me you will live; otherwise, I will not have peace," she gasped.

"I promise, Mum." It was the last thing he spoke before the drugs kicked in, and he fell asleep before arriving at the hospital.

.

CHAPTER 21- COMING TO TERMS WITH THE PAST

Brady slammed his fists into the wall, causing the window to clatter as the horror of that night grabbed hold of him.

"NO, NO, NO!" he yelled, punching the wall repeatedly, each blow more forceful than the last.

Sara jumped out of her peaceful slumber, frightened, and rushed into Brady's room to see what was all the raucous. The sight should have scared her, but somehow, she felt sorrow filled her. Without thinking, she rushed to his side.

"Brady! Stop, *please!*" her voice broke into a sob.

With ragged breaths, he withdrew his clenched fists. Brady turned his head in her direction and stared at her with creased brows. Pain reflected from his eyes as the tears cascaded down his cheeks.

"It's . . . all . . . my fault she died, Sara!" he

wailed, unable to accept the truth from the memories he'd just had.

"Who are you talking about?" Sara whispered.

Brady unclenched his fists, raised his right hand to his face, and wiped the tears from his cheeks before he faced her fully.

"My mum," he let out, sounding defeated.

Sara gasped and blurted. "Brady, there is blood all over your face!"

He raised his hands in the light that reflected in the room from the moonlight to stare at his knuckles, which had begun to sting, blood covering them.

"You've busted those real bad, Brady! Just . . . just stay still. I'll be right back."

Sara switched on one of his bedside lamps then sprinted into his bathroom, grabbed a washrag, some water, and the first-aid kit. With everything clutched in her arms, she hurried back into Brady's bedroom, trying not to spill any of the water as she goes. Brady sat on the floor by the window with his back leant against the wall, a dazed look stuck to his face accompanied by tears.

Sara sat down next to him, "Brady." His eyes met hers. "I'm going to wash the blood from your hands and dress the wounds, okay?"

He said nothing, only lowered his gaze.

Sara laid the basin of water on her lap, then gently lifted Brady's right hand and dipped it into the water. He winced at the contact but gave her no resistance as she began to wash the blood away with the washcloth.

Sara dried his hand and laid it on his leg

before she repeated the process with his left. After removing the basin from her lap and laying it aside, she reached for the first-aid kit and pulled out a tube of antibiotic ointment. She squeezed a small amount on her fingertip and gently massaged it on Brady's knuckles, after which she wrapped them in bandages.

Tears clouded Sara's eyes as she watched Brady. He looked so defeated. An image of her father sitting on his bed in the dark flashed before her. Her heart began to pound hard, panic set in, and she froze.

Her stillness caused Brady to lift his gaze to see the fear in her eyes.

"Sara," he whispered.

No answer. He reached to touch her shoulder but withdrew, uncertain of how she would react.

"Sara, I would never hurt you or do anything to you like your dad or those other men," he croaked.

Sara blinked at the mention of her father and stared into Brady's eyes.

"You should go back to bed, Sara—I will be fine." He tried to smile.

Sara reached for the washbasin and squeezed the water from the washrag.

"Leave it, Sara."

She ignored him and raised it to his cheek. Fresh tears streamed down Brady's face, making the mixture of blood and tears remind her of seeing women crying with makeup on.

"Sara, please just go. I can finish doing it myself. I can't bear you seeing me anything like your father."

Sara took a deep breath and began to wipe

the smear from his face. "I don't see you like that, Brady," she finally said. "I just panicked for a moment; if I saw you as my father, I would have run from you."

"Sara!" his voice raised a bit, and his eyes widened, "You saw how I've dealt with knowing I'm responsible for my mum's death. I don't want you to have to relive any more of your past."

"Brady, I'm not leaving you like this."

Sara didn't wait for him to protest further and proceeded to clean his face.

"I'll be right back," she said in a gentle tone and smiled.

Sara stood to her feet, took the washrag, the basin, and the first-aid kit back into the bathroom, and then headed downstairs to the kitchen. She took a glass from the cupboard and filled it with tap water, then went back to Brady.

"I got you some water."

She stretched the glass towards him, then sat back down next to him. He awkwardly held the glass and drank it all without taking a breath.

"Thank you, Sara," Brady said, taking a deep breath.

"Why did you say it's your fault your mum died, Brady?" she asked, concerned.

He sighed. "When I ended up in Lexington, I suppressed all the painful and depressing memories I had in my life. Tonight, after listening to you, I could not sleep. All the memories I hid surfaced, preventing me from getting any sleep and forcing me to face them. I discovered it was my fault Mum died. She died after a few days in the hospital because of her fall; it caused internal bleeding. We both fell, but she died, and I lived. I had suffered knowing all this happened because the house caught fire from a joint that fell from my hand when I fell asleep, and now I have to relive it."

Sara pulled Brady's head against her shoulder and let him weep: finally accepting what happened. She knew it would be harder for him to get past his past than she would hers, and she vowed to be there for him always.

"Come, Brady; see if you can get some sleep," Sara said after a couple of minutes. She stood and helped him to his feet.

Brady walked over to his bed and slipped beneath the covers, allowing Sara to tuck in the edges around him before she walked to the door.

"Goodnight, Brady," she smiled.

Brady smiled back, and a look of peace covered his face. "Goodnight, Sara, and thank you," he told her, then closed his eyes.

Sara nodded and closed the door behind her as she left his room and went back to bed.

Over the next couple of days, Brady did not say much about what he remembered. However, as he observed Sara's supportive and caring attitude towards him, he began to share with her everything he remembered little by little during their dinnertime.

Relief blossomed within him, seeing that her affection was not hindered by what he shared. This gave him the courage to show her all his paintings, now ten in total. As Sara stared at each one, she could almost feel the agony he felt from his past. Even though they depicted darkness, pain, and torment, they were very good.

"Brady, don't dispose of these paintings as yet. I sense you should hold on to them for a while," she suggested.

"All right, Sara, I kind of have that feeling, too. Help me put them back into the storage room till we figure out why that is," he asked and smiled.

Since that day, colours have found expression in his paintings. Life felt more joyful to him; even his paintings reflected it.

For the next couple of months of them living together, they grew to accept each other as family and enjoyed being around each other. Sara continued to spend the mornings around the piano writing new songs. She'd entertain herself by playing her favourites tunes while Brady continued with his painting. After dinner, they usually found themselves entertaining each other by playing music and singing together, laughing, and watching movies, which they both had come to enjoy together.

Every Wednesday afternoon, they would break from what they were doing to go into town and purchase groceries and whatever else they needed to replenish. Sara noticed that each time they went into town, each homeless person Brady saw he would excuse himself and return with a meal. Then he would hand it to that person, even sometimes giving them some money.

She wondered if it had something to do with the condition in which he met her that brought this out in him. As much as she wanted to ask him the first time, she waited to see if it was something he would keep doing.

After arriving back home one evening from doing their usual Wednesday shopping, they sat relaxed on the porch drinking some cool pineapple juice. Sara could not keep herself from the suspense anymore and asked. "Brady, why do you give food to homeless people each time you see one in town? Is it because of me that you do it?"

"What?" his brows arched in surprise. "No, Sara, it's not because of you. It's just that every time I see someone there, I remember when I lived on the streets and some of the things I endured."

"You told me you lived on the streets, but never told me why."

Brady took a deep breath and stared at her. "After Mum died, everything went downhill for me, and it was far worse than when John had died. I could not focus on work, and now I had no place to stay. My promise to Mum was what kept me from ending it all. Shawn and Denise kept asking me to come to stay with them in Miami, but I refused, knowing Dad would certainly blame me for Mum's death."

"Was that when you ended up on the streets?"

"No, one of my work colleagues let me sleep on his couch during that time, but after a few weeks, I finally gave in to Shawn's pleading. When I got to Miami, being around Shawn helped take some of the hurt away, and I wanted to see Denise—she was like a mum to me and always understood me. I called her and told her I was coming by one morning when Dad was at the store, and she was ecstatic. She told me not to worry about him and that she would talk to him. Shawn offered to accompany me just in case something caused my dad to be at the house when I turned up, and trouble arose—I agreed.

"Shawn is such a protector," Brady chuckled to himself. "He told me to wait at my dad's gate and ran up the steps to the front door. He knocked to ensure that it was Denise, who answered the door."

"Was it her?" Sara asked curiously.

"Yes, and she dashed out and gave me such a tight squeeze, I gasped for air. I felt such joy seeing her face and feeling that motherly love. She kept telling me to not blame myself for Mum's death and that I should not stay away. However, soon after telling me all that, I heard a loud stomping from inside the house, heading towards the front door, and immediately, I knew my dad was there . . . ."

"What did he do?"

Brady smiled at Sara. "Sara," he said in a soft voice, "just listen. If you keep interrupting me, I might forget what I want to say. Dad stood at the front door and glared at me with such fierceness—all I could think about was our last tussle. Soon, he could not contain his silence and began to spit out everything he wanted to tell me." Brady sighed at the thought before continuing. "He said, 'I was a no-good son, who only seemed to excel at being a disappointment to everyone around him.' I kissed Denise on the cheek, then Shawn and I left—that was the last time I saw them.

"I spent six months helping Shawn on the farm, and it brought me some peace. It was hard work, too, but it kept my mind from dwelling on the past. I spent every moment I had working on the farm; Shawn had to ask me to take it easy a few times."

Sara smiled.

"A phone call, which came at the end of those six months, changed the course of my life and what led to me ending up on the street, then to Lexington." Sara's mouth opened as if ready to pose a question, and Brady eyed her.

"Sorry," she said and smiled.

"My friend, Ricky—who was at St. Peter's with me—and Shawn called and mentioned he was thinking of joining the Navy. Shawn urged me to join as well, as a way to fulfil what John and I wanted. I agreed. I figured, for everything that had gone wrong in my life, this was the perfect way of making things right and honouring both John and Mum's memory.

"When Ricky and I sent in our applications, we almost got rejected when they did our background checks and found we were at St. Peters. If not for Major Stalker—sorry, habit—Matron Bull's intervention and recommendation, we wouldn't have gotten in.

"Those eight weeks of physical training were gruelling, but we loved it. The drills and academic tests were a breeze, and we came out with flying colours come graduation day. Dad didn't show. Denise said he felt too ashamed for how he acted when I came to see her. Gram came with her bright smile and positive words—telling me to stop seeing myself as a failure and be proud. When I received that certificate, I was proud, thinking it was John and me up there. It was a great milestone moment for me.

"Those two years in the Navy, out at sea, with one of my best friends, made me believe in a good future in the Navy. We were trained to be hull technicians, and it kept us busy doing something important."

Brady smiled, and for a few seconds, his eyes grew distant, then went silent. Sara, though eager to know what was running through his head, managed to sit still and wait until he was ready to speak again. He took a deep breath and stared into her eyes.

"A fire broke out on the ship in one of the cargo compartments. My fire team was closest at hand when the report was made, so we went to fight the fire . . ."

"Fight the fire?" she asked with creased brows.

"It's a Navy term." He chuckled and continued. "After we isolated the fire area, my team proceeded into the compartment while our backup team followed behind us. Once we were inside the compartment, we saw it a Class A fire..."

"Ugh?" Sara's brows creased in perplexity. "Layman's term, Brady."

Brady chuckled. "Sorry. The Navy classifies fires into three categories: Class A fires are from wood, bedding, paper, and ammunition; Class B is from fuel and lubricants, and Class C is electrical. Got it?"

She nodded.

"Good. I was one of the hosemen, and as we applied foam to the fire, it began to roar fiercely. I found myself staring into the eyes of a deadly enemy, and I froze. The horror of the day Mum and I almost perished in the fire flashed before me. I don't remember what happened next except that I was up on deck and Ricky saying something I couldn't hear. I mean, I heard him, but my mind was distant so nothing made sense. I got sent to a treatment hospital, and after the psychologist assessed and diagnosed my situation, he determined that I needed psychological treatment and that the Navy wasn't where I needed to be at that time, so I was medically discharged," he sighed. "Ricky knew I beat myself up about not being able to fulfil my role in diffusing the fire and told me on the day I headed home that none of the men perished—that only a few suffered heat exhaustion and smoke inhalation, and that it wasn't my fault. It was a tough enemy, so he says."

Brady gulped down the rest of his juice and took a deep breath before he continued. "Shawn and Denise wanted me to come back to Miami, and Gram wanted me to stay with her out here, but when I thought about all the disasters that followed me, I didn't want to take a chance to be around anyone I loved—for fear of losing anyone else. I rejected their offers, and instead, headed to the burnt-out remains of the house, where Mum and I had lived."

CHAPTER 22- HITTING ROCK BOTTOM

"I stood at the foot of the steps to the house, and it made me cringe. I felt anger rising in me for Mum's death. I hated marijuana and drugs, even alcohol—though I wasn't a drinker.

"When I mounted the steps and walked into the burnt-out remains, I craved so much to feel Mum's presence there . . . to take the hurt away, but only emptiness and coldness surrounded me. When I walked through that house, everything was gone except the old-fashioned wardrobe in my mum's room. It was what I curled up in night after night and slept."

Sara could not contain herself any longer and waited until Brady ended his story. "How did you eat when you cut yourself off from everyone?" she blurted.

Brady only smiled. "Denise, Gram, and Shawn all offered to send me money since I refused to stay with them; Shawn wouldn't take no for an answer and threatened to come and get me if I failed to accept his help. The thing is, Sara; you might be thinking why I didn't get a place to live if I was getting help, but I felt as if darkness followed me, and I couldn't bear causing anyone harm by my presence.

"I wanted to die as much as you did when you went through your trauma. Mum's words were what kept me from ending it all. Every day, I tried to think of happy times I spent with John and Mum until the memories gave me headaches. I started sketching bits of the images from my mind on the walls until I bought a sketchpad and a pencil. I drew every good memory that I remembered, and each day, I would relive those moments through those sketches.

"Two months later, the owners of the ruin came to rebuild and chased me off the property. That's when I began to wander the streets. I never stayed at one location for too long. I'd often get unpleasant stares from persons. Somehow my quiet persona and clean appearance made me an easy target for the scoundrels, who went around robbing others. They would always be so shocked when the force of my fists collided with their cheeks. I must have gotten in a fight every other week and had to always be on my guard because of them. However, in the midst of all that, whenever I found a quiet spot, I would stay there and sketch—that gave me peace.

"Four months had passed, and I was officially twenty-two. I felt the need to hear familiar voices and called Shawn, Denise, and

Grams. Hearing their voices made me feel like I could start over. However, two days after my birthday, an event occurred that landed me in Lexington and crushed my dream of starting over."

"What happened?" Sara asked anxiously.

"Are you sure you want to know?"

"Please," she nodded.

"Okay. Since all my valuables were in my backpack, I usually used it as a pillow to protect my stuff. No one ever tried to snatch my bag, as that would wake me up, and we would end up in a tussle. But one person did, and when I felt the tug beneath my neck and opened my eyes, it was to the sight of a huge, bald man, standing over me with piercing eyes. When I yanked my bag back, he punched me in the face and then tried to strangle me. When he saw that he had the upper hand, he removed one hand from my throat and began to untwine my hand from the bag's strap.

"He was such a big guy that it was hard to fight him off. All I could do was reach for something to hit him with. A rock that lay close to my knee came to my rescue, and while he was distracted, fighting to remove my hand from the bag, I grabbed that rock. Then I mustered all my strength and struck him hard across the face the minute he turned to face me again before I pushed him off me.

"I didn't even give myself time to recover from almost being choked to death. I got up and pushed him to the ground as he staggered about from the blow he sustained. I stood and took two deep breaths to gain some strength and then kicked him hard in the stomach and his face. My cup of bitterness was full from all the harrassment I had encountered on the streets. The man's face bled hard, but I did not care; I kept kicking him everywhere until he passed out.

"As I lumped down next to him, staring at his unconscious body, I took up the rock and held over his face, wanting to smash his face and end it all, but voices that shouted in the distance caused me to drop it.

"Surveillance cameras, which were placed on street poles to clamp down on violent acts in that area, were what saved me from getting a longer sentence. Even though the footage showed that the man attacked me first, the judge sentenced me to seven years because the man ended up in a coma. I heard he stayed in the hospital for a year. The judge said the rage that I had deemed me unfit to be put back on the streets and that I needed to be somewhere I can be put to good use."

"Brady, I'm sorry you went through all that." Sara reached for his hand and gently squeezed. "I know it must have been hard to accept your mum's death, hearing what your dad said about you, and thinking yourself unfit to be around those you love. I bet you even thought God was far from you, too."

"I did, Sara," he sighed. "I thought all my actions deserved his separation."

"But, in all that despair, you had people who loved you and offered to help you any way they could while giving you space to grieve and come to terms with it all. God allowed you to find joy in your art and gave you peace while surrounded by wolves. That, alone, should have shown you that He was always with you. And having peace is a sure sign of his presence with us. How many persons quit life going through what you went through, or even worse, went crazy? You endured it all." Sara told him with optimism, causing him to smile as he stared at her. "What?" she asked, blushing by the look she saw in his eyes.

"You just remind me so much of her—Mum, I mean. She always tried to see good in everything, which was why I loved her so much. She was my strength and biggest motivator. I'm glad you're here, Sara. Somehow having you here has made life pleasant, and you have come to mean a lot to me, too," he said, still smiling. He did not feel so wounded anymore. Talking about his past with Sara gave him so much peace that he didn't feel the need to hold anything back. She understood him and accepted him.

Sara smiled back. Her heart began to beat fast, and it made her feel somewhat nervous. She knew she had come to care a lot for Brady, after knowing so much about him. She saw how he took her into his home and cared for her without asking anything in return. She wasn't sure what to make of it, though.

"Sara, could you do me a favour?"

"Sure, Brady."

"I want to go see my mum's grave. Will you accompany me?"

"Of course.

"I didn't have the courage to face her since we've been here. I wasn't ready, but now that I have relieved myself of carrying the past around, I would like to."

"It would be a good way to close that chapter

and embrace your new beginning as I am now doing as well."

He nodded. "You are right. Are you up for it today? It's not far from here; it's about twenty minutes in the same direction as the river—just a little detour."

"Sounds good to me, and it would be nice to see the rest of this beautiful countryside—and with you, too." She blushed, feeling a flutter inside her.

Brady stood to his feet and pulled Sara up from her chair, "Let's go, then." He led her off the porch and out of the house.

CHAPTER 23- GETTING ACQUAINTED

Beads of sweat trickled down Brady and Sara's faces as they trekked downhill through the dirt tracks towards the family plot.

"I'm sorry, Sara," Brady breathed as he wiped his face with the back of his hand. "I forgot how hot it gets along this path."

Sara wiped the sweat droplets from her nose and forehead and flicked it off her hand.

"Don't worry; we're almost there. There are quite a few shady trees to rest under and enjoy the fresh air," Brady added.

This made Sara smile.

Brady pulled back the latch on the iron gate and swung the gate wide open, allowing Sara to step inside. He then reached for her hand, and she blushed, unresisting. It brought her joy knowing Brady needed her—she wanted to support him as much as he'd been supporting her.

Sara counted three more graves as she and Brady ambled towards his mother's grave: his grandparent's and brother's. The moment they stood in front of Claudette's grave, she felt Brady go tense.

Claudette Fraser—born 1950 and died in 2000.

She was only fifty years old, Sara thought to herself as she read the gravestone. She glanced up at Brady and trailed his eyes to the dried-up flowers, which lay on top of the tombstone. Turning her eyes back to his, she caught a glimpse of the single tear that slipped from his eye—she knew he was trying to hold it together.

"Brady, it's time to let go," she whispered.

He turned his head to face her and gave her a little smile.

"How do I let go, Sara? It was so hard when John died. Mum was there to help me through that. How will I get past losing her, knowing now that it was my fault?" he asked in a sombre tone.

Sara placed her other hand on top of his hand that held hers and stared up into his eyes, eyes she thought looked so kind.

"I will help you, Brady," she smiled.

Brady smiled back.

It was as if a veil lifted from Sara's eyes, allowing her to see his handsome features for the first time. His eyes and smile lit up, fluttering her heart.

"I appreciate that, Sara, and thank you for coming with me, too," he told her before he returned his gaze to his mother's grave. "I love you, Mum, and as I promised you, I will live for all of us and keep your love in my heart. It took me a long time to let go of the hurt, but I am finally at that place where I am ready." He squeezed Sara's hand and glanced at her with a smile before glancing back at the grave. "And today, Mum, I'm closing the door to the past and accepting that everyone deserves second chances. I now embrace mine. *Oh*, I almost forgot to mention that I am painting again. The first set would scare you a bit, but you would have understood each one. Now I am painting with so much joy, you would smile seeing each one; I know Gram would. It was always her wish for me to paint again, and I'm happy she didn't give up on me, Mum, just like you never did. Goodbye, Mum."

Brady held onto Sara's hand as he stepped away from his mother's grave and headed towards the gate. Just before they exited the burial ground, Sara's eye caught sight of another grave.

"Brady, whose grave is that?" She pulled him towards it.

"That's Mr. Walsh. He and Grandpa bought this land together for their families. They were the best of friends growing up together in Philadelphia."

"So, Mr. Walsh was Irish, too?"

"Yes. Both his parents and Grandpa's parents were Irish immigrants, who came over when the great plague hit Ireland, which caused millions to starve to death there. But they discovered that it was just as hard here for many immigrants who had no skills and had to take whatever jobs they could get at whatever wages offered. Other immigrants that lived there hated them for that and would place racist signs in their business establishments, like, 'No Irish needed here,' which I believe is the reason many ended up in mental institutions."

"That's harsh; people can be so cruel."

"That's true, good thing my grandpa and Mr. Walsh's parents were good blacksmiths and streamstresses, who secured good jobs that enabled them to support their families."

"Why did they come out here while you guys stayed behind?"

"Well, both men wanted to escape from the harsh treatments Irish Citizens received in comparison to others. Even when they became adults, it was still very much a problem. They wanted their kids to travel with them, but their kids were married and found it hard to leave without their spouses, who were not willing to leave since they had no problems. So, Grandpa and Mr. Walsh took all their savings, came out here with their wives, bought land next to each other, and built their houses, hoping to leave an inheritance for their kids."

"And their dreams have come true—well, your grandpa's, that is. Since you have now accepted it and care for it," Sara added.

"Yes, the Bible did say that 'a good man leaves an inheritance for his children,' and I'm glad Grandpa did. I truly love it here; I did not like Philadelphia that much. Thanks, a lot Grandpa." Brady glanced around the burial ground. "Let go," he added and led Sara through the gate, shutting it behind them.

"Sara, would you take a swim by the river with me? It's such a hot day, and a swim would be so nice about now; or do you still not trust me to go swimming with me?"

"I do trust you, Brady, but are we to go swimming in what we're wearing?"

"Sure, makes it more fun. Come on," he laughed and pulled her along.

Five minutes later, they stood on the wooden planks at the river bank, where swimmers usually sat, relaxing with their feet in the water. Sara sat down and began to remove her shoes while Brady kicked off his one by one. As soon as he got them off, he pulled his shirt over his head, and Sara's eyes widened.

"Relax, I'm just removing my shirt. I don't want it sticking to my face while I'm swimming. You don't have to worry about yours, it's close-fitting, so you won't have any problem," he smirked.

Sara's eyes ogled Brady's muscular chest. She had never been in a position before to admire the perfect frame of a man's upper torso.

"You like?" Brady teased when he noticed her eyeing him.

Sara's face turned red.

"I got this at Lexington," he flexed his muscles and laughed.

Sara giggled and stood up. "You're so silly, Brady."

"I know," Brady chuckled, and very swiftly he scooped her up into his arms.

"Brady, put me down!" Sara squealed and twisted in his arms.

Brady laughed, walking closer to the edge, and jumped into the water, making a big splash. The moment they touched the cool water, they both laughed.

"Wow, this feels so rejuvenating," he said aloud.

"It sure feels refreshing after that heat," Sara added.

They swam and laughed, freeing themselves of all the pain they once held onto. Brady loved being around Sara, she brought a smile to his face every time. He felt such warmness in his heart for her. He knew he cared for her a lot and wanted to protect her, but he wondered if what he now felt was more than just that.

As he stared at her, he found himself looking at her differently than he usually did, and his heart pitter-pattered. He saw a glow on her face as she smiled back at him. Without thinking, he raised his hands to her face and cupped her cheeks. She closed her eyes, surrendering to his touch as he leaned in and kissed her lips.

"Brady, I'm scared," Sara, told him after he eased from the kiss.

"Me, too, Sara, but it feels right with you, and I want you. I could never do to you what your dad and those other men did to you either."

"I know that, but I don't want to rush into anything and lose you. You're all I have, Brady," she told him as her eyes became moist.

"Oh, come here, you won't lose me, Sara. It's you who brings light to my life now. How could I let you go? And I'm not in any haste either, so don't worry." Brady pulled her into his arms, held her close, and pressed a kiss atop her head. "Let's go back to the house before we start to shiver. It's getting chilly now," he added.

"Good idea."

As time passed, their relationship grew. They supported each other and enjoyed being with each other, even if away from the world by themselves. Quite often, they would pay a visit to Mrs. Walsh, whom Brady had introduced Sara to shortly after she had arrived; they would spend a few hours with her every other day. Mrs. Walsh always welcomed the company since she now lived alone. Brady appreciated how much she had honoured his grandmother's wishes concerning him.

Sara loved getting to know Mrs. Walsh but found herself getting rather curious each time she and Brady dropped in on Mrs. Walsh and Clara's name came up. She knew that Clara was Mrs. Walsh's granddaughter, whom she hadn't heard from in months it seemed. What bugged her was why Brady always asked about her.

"Brady, why is it that every time you and I go to visit Mrs. Walsh, you ask about her granddaughter?" she asked him one evening at dinner.

"Someone sounds jealous," he chuckled, "don't be jealous of someone whom I have not seen since I was fourteen? So much has happened since then and she only liked John that way. I just ask out of curiosity, being that we were close childhood friends."

He stood up from his chair, walked around the table to where Sara sat, stooped down next to her, and spun her chair to face him.

"Listen, Sara, God didn't allow me to go through all that mess, which led me to find you, only for me to walk away from you for someone I knew when I was fourteen. *Do you not know how much you mean to me yet?"* he emphasised, caressing her cheek.

Sara smiled and wrapped her arms around Brady's neck; he pulled her close and stared into her soft eyes.

"I do know, Brady; I just wanted to hear you say it, I'm sorry."

Brady placed a soft kiss to her cheek, then pressed his forehead against hers. "No need to apologise."

Later that night while Sara brushed her teeth to prepare for bed, she could feel God smiling down at her at the thought of how much Brady cared for her. He had not told her he loved her, but she felt it deep inside her heart. She saw it in his eyes and felt it in his kiss.

She practically danced her way out of the bathroom and back into the bedroom as she headed towards the dresser. She pulled open the top drawer and dug through it in search of her nightdress. Not finding it there, she found herself going through drawer after drawer.

"Now where could it be?"

She ambled over to the closet, although she hardly ever used it, except to get a fresh towel. It was where Brady had told her he stored them, but it was the only other place left to search. She opened the closet and dug through all the towels.

Her brows knitted in surprise. "What's this?" She lifted the last towel and stared at a large chest of some kind. "How come I never noticed this before?"

Sara scooped up all the towels in her arms and tossed them on her bed, then dragged the huge chest from the closet.

"Wow, it's so beautiful," she said as she walked around the chest, examining it.

It was carved wood. As soon as her eyes caught sight of a lock with a key in it, she knelt in front of the box.

"I guess this must belong to Brady's grandmother since this was her room. The initials below this keyhole here looked like hers."

Sara bit her bottom lip for a moment, pondering if it would be invading her privacy, seeing she's no longer alive. "I wonder if Brady even knows about this box."

Her curiosity bit her hard.

"I don't think she'll mind if I take a look. I'll just tell Brady about it afterwards and hope he won't get upset."

Sara's eyes widened as she lifted the lid and saw many of Brady's letters addressed to his grandmother. There were also photos of his young grandparents and other special memorabilia. It touched her heart, seeing how sentimental his grandmother was.

Sara's attention was then drawn back to Brady's letters—there were so many, all organised by year. She picked up the bundle, which held the earliest letters and scrutinised them: *Lexington prison 2003.* She tucked the bundle of letters under her arm, closed the chest lid, got up, and walked over to her bed.

As eager as she was to start reading them, she did not feel her room would be the best place to do so. She decided the next day that she would go down to the burial ground, sit under one of the cool trees, and read there while Brady painted.

Sara turned to the nightstand to place the

bundle of letters down before she went to put the chest back into the closet, and smiled when she noticed the bulge beneath the sheets. She set the letters down on the nightstand and then plucked back the cover from the bed.

"Ah, I must have been in a hurry this morning to make my bed and not see you there," she said to the nightdress as she picked it up.

Tossing the nightdress over her shoulder, she walked back to the chest, lifted it, and placed it back into the closet. However, she decided to place the towels into a vacant drawer in the chest of drawers so she would be able to access the chest better.

As she dressed in her nightdress, she smiled anxiously to start reading Brady's letters.

CHAPTER 24- DISCOVERING LEXINGTON AND GETTING BUSTED

Lexington April 2003,
 Dear Gram,
 It has been nearly seven months since I've been here now, and it feels like hell. Every day, we wake up at 7:00 a.m. They feed us a good breakfast only to have us fit for the day's work. They take us to a work site, where we have to break rocks like how you see in those old prison movies. By the time we get back, we only have the strength to shower, eat, and sleep—to start the process again the next day.
 I feel nothing, Gram; all my joy, hopes, everything is gone. Nothing matters anymore. Sometimes the guards are so mean, even when they see us struggling under the weight of those heavy rocks, and the sun beats against our

already battered bodies. I could not hold my anger last week when one of the guards pushed me and caused me to hit my head against the pile of rocks I was breaking. I picked up one and slammed it against his chest, causing him to fall. They locked me in isolation for three weeks because he ended up in the hospital. I didn't even care, Gram. Is this the person you see light in?

Lexington June 2003,
   Dear Gram,
   Today, I was attacked by three prisoners because I beat up a mate who spoke about my mum. He had the nerve to say she must have been a whore to produce a son like me. I cannot stand hearing anyone speaking badly about Mum. Now I'm nursing a bruised jaw, swollen eye, and sore legs, and I still have to get up and work tomorrow. They don't care about you if you were in fights; you still have to go and work. I think the guards sometimes set the other prisoners to attack me because of the time I hurt that guard. They have been watching me ever since.

   Since the incident with the guard, the other guards don't harass me out there; they wait until we're back here, and each time either they or the prisoners would attack me, I would give it to them hard. Solitary has become like home to me here, and somehow, I find I don't mind it compared to being around them. I hate them, Gram. I almost choked a man to death last week. I think I have lost total control of my temper now, Gram. I don't know if your prayers can save me anymore.

Sara burst into tears when she read the letters, feeling Brady's pain. Each day, she would go out to the burial ground and read at least three letters. She didn't want to get too consumed and lose track of time. That would alert Brady to look for her, only to discover she's reading them.

Lexington January 2004,
Dear Gram,

Everyone avoids me now like the plague. They are tired of the wounds I inflict on them when they attack me, and I am glad for the break, too. I like the solitude, and I work more without the constant harassment. Got a letter from Shawn last week, and he's taking my being here hard. Can you call him and encourage him for me as you always do me? I can't handle knowing he's walking around with such weight when he has his mum and aunt to care for, please, Gram. How are you? Thank you for your card and your encouraging words. I tried writing to Dad as you suggested, but it has been three weeks and no reply. I think I will try again next month. I know how stubborn and prideful he can be. Take care of yourself, Gram.

Lexington July 2004,
Dear Gram,

I think I am finally coming to terms that I will never be able to live a happy, normal life, even after coming out. Who will ever want to love someone like me after learning about this past of mine? I don't even think I'm someone worthy of God's forgiveness, even though you said in the

Bible that, in 1 John, it says, ' That if I confess my sins, He is faithful and just to forgive me and cleanse me from all my sins.' It just seems too good to believe that he would want me into His kingdom and family. Look at the disaster I've caused to the one life he gave me.

Will His angels want to watch over me? They might fear my temper, too, and avoid me like the plague like everyone. Sorry, Gram, that was a joke. However, I am trying to change, although it's hard to see any good to look forward to; that is worth even trying. You are the only light left in my life, and I am scared to even come around me when I get out, so no harm will come to you. Oh, before I forget, I tried Dad again, and he still hasn't answered and that's the third letter I wrote.

Lexington August 2005,
Dear Gram,

Happy birthday! Hope you had a good one and spent it well with Mrs. Walsh. You two have always been like sisters. I have some good news, Gram. Dad finally replied to my letter and said he accepted my apology and that he's sorry, too, for all the things he said about me. He sends his love from him and Denise. And I also got a letter from Shawn who told me that Mr. Jones died two months ago and left him everything. He also said his mum is doing well and better from her stroke.

I am so happy for him, and his letter gave me hope that maybe I can be happy when I get out of here. If God can forgive me, maybe he will have someone out there who will love me after knowing everything about me. These days, I find

I don't feel so angry anymore, and I find I want to be happy. I prayed to God one night in my cell and asked him to forgive me for everything I ever did wrong, and since then, I have been feeling somehow freer from all the rage. Although it tries to overcome me at times, I find I can control it as I have no desire to hold on to hate anymore. I miss smiling and feeling love and joy and even just the laughter of a friend. Such things many take for granted seem so precious to me, locked away in here. I have even tried reaching out to some of the prisoners, who are very suspicious of me, but they will see I'm trying in time. I love you, Gram.

Bye for now.

"Sara!" Brady shouted as he entered the burial ground and saw her sitting under a shady tree, caught up in reading something.

The sound of her name caused Sara to jump in fright, and clumsily, she refolded the letter. She glanced about, tempted to hide it from him, but as she watched him walk towards her with a smile, she knew it meant he trusted her. She decided she would never lie to him or betray his trust. Her heart pounded as he approached.

"What are you doing out here?" he exhaled and sat down next to her. "Did you get a letter from your dad?" he asked, seeing the letter in her hand.

"Brady," she breathed, "I . . . I have something to tell you, and I am not sure how you will react."

His eyes squinted in curiosity. "What is it, Sara? Did you get bad news?"

"No," she nodded and stretched the letter to him. "I found the letters you wrote to your grandmother."

"You were scared that I would be mad that you read them?"

She nodded.

Brady smiled and squeezed her hand. "I'm not mad. I'm glad you did; you saved me the trouble of talking about those dark years."

Sara breathed a sigh of relief. "You're not? I'm still sorry I went through your grandmother's things without telling you first; it's not a quality I want you to see in me. Thank you for not being upset."

"Sara, . . . it's alright."

She smiled. "I found them in my closet three months ago. There were so many, but I only got to where you gave your life to Christ and started reaching out to the other prisoners."

"Well, it gets better from there; I went around and apologised to everyone, including the guards. At first, they all wondered if being in isolation so often had caused me to start going crazy. However, when they saw that I did not resort back to my old ways, they realised I was sincere. Many forgave me after they allowed me to relate to them—how I ended up becoming that violent.

"Before long, many of them were coming to me to ask me how I overcame the rage and managed to transform myself. That's when I found myself sharing about how my Gram was always praying for me and how no matter what, she never gave up on me. I told them how she often encouraged me through scriptures, which she always wrote at the end of every letter. Soon, I found myself teaching them the very verses that had helped me change and now see myself as the new man I became in Christ. That was when I first got to watch a movie while in prison and use the library.

"The prison warden wanted me to stay on as a counsellor because he saw how effective my talks were to the prisoners, which led to a reduction in fights. I told him maybe, but for now, I needed to get my life together first. Sara, when I got to Lexington, I saw it in a negative light, but with several years of soul-searching, sobriety, and self-discovery, I now see this whole experience for what it is. It's the most positive experience of my life up until now by far. *I wasn't arrested; I was rescued.*"

Brady took a deep breath and continued. "Sara, I was thinking that maybe it is time for you to call your dad and see how he is doing. I have a feeling he might need to see you soon. It's just a gut feeling I've had since last night. By the way, you never told me what your dad's name is."

Sara laughed. "Sorry about that; his name is George Anderson. I will call him when we get back to the house. Are you ready to go back now? Or do you want to stay here and enjoy the cool breeze a bit longer?

"No rush." Brady lay on the grass with his head on Sara's lap. "Sing me a song, Sara," he said, staring up into her eyes.

Sara ran her fingers through his hair, and a broad smile spread across her face as she began to sing him one of the songs she wrote that was now his favourite. His eyes sparkled as he kept her gaze through the entire song.

As the song ended, Sara reached for Brady's hand and entwined her fingers with his. She brought his hand to her lips and kissed it before lowering it back to his chest. With a smile in her eyes, she pressed a gentle kiss on his cheek before she whispered in his ear. "I appreciate you so much Brady."

"And I you, Sara," he whispered back.

An hour later, as they walked back to the house, the sun surrendered, allowing them to enjoy the evening's coolness. Sara looped her hand around Brady's arm, hoping his gut feeling about her dad wasn't something that would devastate her. She was not ready for any bad news just when life seemed to be smiling down at her.

She knew the time would come when she had to face her dad again, and although she wasn't ready, she missed him. Sara glanced up at Brady as they ambled down the beaten path towards the house and smiled. She knew he would support her, giving her the courage to face what was to come. Once they entered the kitchen, she reached for the telephone receiver and dialled her dad's number.

"Hello," George answered firmly.

"Hi, Dad," Sara spoke in a soft tone, "how are you?" Concern itched her voice.

"Sara!" George answered, surprised but happy. "Is that really you, Pumpkin? It's so good to hear your voice," he took a deep breath and continued, "I'm alright. How are you?"

"I am doing okay, Dad."

"I have missed you so much, Pumpkin. I

know you have forgiven me and needed space for healing, but I . . . I long to see you," his voice started to crack.

Sara took a deep breath. "I missed you, too, Dad. I have someplace to stay. I had a gut feeling that something was wrong with you, and I had to find out. So, *Dad*, please tell me if something is."

For about a minute, the line went dead. "Dad! What's wrong?" she asked, growing nervous, which caused Brady, who had started dinner in the kitchen, to run over to find out what the problem was.

"What did he say?" Brady whispered.

"Nothing," she whispered back, covering the receiver.

"I'm sorry, Pumpkin. I . . . I don't want to burden you with this," George finally spoke.

"Dad, *please*, just tell me," she pleaded.

"Alright, well, a couple of months ago, after having trouble urinating, I developed a urinary tract infection. I noticed my prostate enlarged, so I went to see the doctor and discovered that I have what the doctor called a 'Benign Prostatic Hyperplasia.' The doctor tried to treat it with drugs first to ease the flow of my urine, and for a while, it helped. However, my prostate still expanded. The drugs soon became ineffective, so the doctor said the best option is to operate, but . . . there might be complications." He let out a loud exhale. "I have surgery in three days. I sure do miss your mum now."

Sara felt bile crawl up her oesophagus after hearing her dad's words. She knew he was worried, having to go through such an ordeal with his beloved wife dead and his only daughter estranged.

"Dad, . . . don't worry; I'll come home to be with you through the surgery. You will not be alone. I love you very much, Dad."

Sara noticed Brady's face go pale as she spoke of leaving. She hung up the receiver and took hold of his hand, then led him to the dinner table to sit.

"You're leaving?" Brady uttered, sadness laced his voice.

"Brady," her voice was shaky. Sara caressed his cheek, and he closed his eyes under the warmth of her touch. With shallow breaths, she said, "My dad is going to have surgery in three days, and he's all alone and worried." Brady's eyes flew open. "I know I told him I will be there for him, but I don't want to go alone," her voice broke. "Will you please go with me?"

Brady reached for Sara's hand, kissed it, and stroked the back of it. "Sara, I'll go anywhere with you. I'm kind of eager to meet your dad as well." A smile spread across his face. *"Don't worry,* I won't beat up your dad," he chuckled. "You have forgiven him, so that's enough for me, *and* he's repented. I'm happy that you are willing to be with him. After all, that's happened—shows that you have truly forgiven him. And Sara, I'm not letting you out of my sight; I need you just as much as your dad does and even more."

Sara leapt from her chair and into his arms before hugging him tightly. "Thank you. I appreciate your support so much. Oh, Brady, look! The pot is boiling over."

She rushed from his arms and into the kitchen with Brady right behind her to salvage their dinner.

They had a good laugh that night, enjoying the meal they almost lost.

CHAPTER 25- AN OVERDUE REUNION

The next day, they went into town and gathered supplies for the trip to Charleston, West Virginia. Brady packed his sketchpad and pencils to take along to capture inspiring images he saw while getting to know Sara's dad.

Now that he had painted all the darkness out of his system, he wanted to capture all he saw involving Sara. Sara did not question him when she noticed him packing them in his bag. She knew he would need something to occupy his time for a portion of the trip.

They went to bed early that night. Their bus tickets were for 7:00 a.m.; it would take several hours to get to Charleston. Neither had a passport, and there wasn't enough time to apply for one. They slept throughout most of the journey and were famished by the time the bus pulled into the Charleston station. Soon, they refreshed themselves with sandwiches and fruit juice.

Déjà vu kicked in for Sara the minute she stepped out of the taxi; it was of the night she left home. Her feet hesitated as she stared up at the front door from the foot of the steps.

Brady reached for her hand, and she stared up at him.

"It's okay, Sara; I'm here. You don't have to be afraid."

Sara took a deep breath and nodded. "Okay."

Sara followed Brady as he led her up the steps. Brady pressed hard on the door buzzer twice and glanced at Sara, who stood behind him. A few minutes later, they heard the rattling of keys inside the lock.

"Yes, can I help you?" the voice from the man on the other side of the door said.

It was George. Although he had not opened the door wide enough to notice Sara standing there, she saw him. He looked thinner from the last time she'd seen him. As she stared at him, his eyes were still void of the sparkle he once had before her mum's death.

"Are you George Anderson?" Brady asked.

"Who are you?" George brows furrowed in curiosity.

"Dad," Sara spoke up, stepping into his line of sight. It was then that Sara saw a glint of light twinkle in his eyes. Joy filled her heart.

"Pumpkin! You're really here?"

George swung open the door wider to ensure he didn't imagine her. He wanted to hug her so badly but wasn't sure how she would react after what had transpired between them after so many years.

Seeing his anxiety, however, Sara stretched towards him. She gave him a tight embrace, causing him to burst into tears on the spot.

After a few minutes, George composed himself and wiped his tears away with the back of his right sleeve.

"Come on inside," he said, stepping back into the house and led the way.

Brady followed behind George, quite eager to know more about this man but soon realised Sara stood back, frozen at the front door. He spun around in her direction; panic struck her face. With two quick strides, he stood in front of her and gently tilted her chin up to look him in the eyes.

"Sara," he whispered, gripping her attention. "Remember, I'm here. I'm not going anywhere."

Brady gave her a light kiss on the cheek, reached for her hand, and held it firmly in his.

"Ready?" he asked.

Sara squeezed his hand tight and nodded with a weak smile; Brady smiled back and tugged on her hand softly for her to follow him.

George stood halfway into the house watching them, and pain pierced his heart. *My pumpkin's still afraid.* Tears welled up in his eyes as Sara and Brady walked towards him. He smiled, trying to hide his pain, but Sara saw it; she knew her father well enough.

"I'm sorry, Pumpkin," he confessed. "I didn't know coming back here would be this hard for you after so long." He sighed.

"I wasn't sure how I would feel, Dad. I have already forgiven you and wanted to see you and be here for you during the surgery, but I must admit I was scared to come back into this house alone." She turned to Brady. "Dad, this is my friend Brady, Brady, my dad."

Both men stared, scrutinising each other for a few seconds before Brady stretched his hand towards George.

"It's nice to meet you, Sir," he smiled.

George relaxed and smiled back.

"Nice to meet you, too, Brady," George returned Brady's handshake. "Come into the living room, and I'll get you both something to eat or drink. I have lasagna in the fridge I can heat up." He took a step into the living room. "Since you left, Pumpkin, I had to learn how to cook," he chuckled.

Sara smiled back and followed Brady over to the couch, her hand still locked in his as they sat down.

"We're okay for now, Dad; we ate something at the bus station before we got here."

"Alright, well, just relax, Pumpkin. It's still your home, and you, too, young man." George sat down on the chair closest to Sara and leaned back. "So, Brady, what do you do?"

"I'm an artist; I paint. Sara told me you're a policeman and that you come from a long line of men in uniform."

"That's right, all the men in my family have served either in the military or the police force from as far back as I can remember," George confirmed with a little smile. "What about your family?" he probed, hoping to learn as much about the man who managed to bring his daughter back home. He needed to know if Brady was good enough for his daughter. Though, in his mind, he rendered himself unworthy to even claim who's right or wrong for her. He could not help it; she was still his pumpkin, and he wanted the best for her.

"My family—everyone's dead except my dad and step-mum." Brady's eyes darted around the room. He didn't want to get too deep into his family life with a stranger, no less someone who may not understand the struggles he went through.

"Dad, what time is your surgery scheduled for tomorrow?" Sara imputed, realising Brady wasn't too keen to talk about his family with her dad.

George and Brady turned to face her now.

"It's at 9:00 a.m., Pumpkin, and to be honest, I'm nervous. Your mother used to know how to make everything easier. I still miss her so much," he sighed.

Sara reached for her dad's hand and sandwiched it between hers. She didn't see him as the man who had hurt her but the father she had loved very much. She wanted him to see that she was committed to being there for him.

"Dad, trust me when I say I forgive you and have left all that had happened between us in the past. I know you feel like I won't stay after the surgery to help you get back on your feet because of everything. But I hold no bitterness towards you, and Brady had a lot to do with that, too," she told him, glancing over at Brady.

George's eyes widened in disbelief, and he became pale. Mortified, he stared past Sara over to Brady, whose face showed no signs of animosity.

"You knew, and yet you shook my hand," he took a deep breath and continued, not giving Brady a chance to answer.

"I hated myself for so long. I even wanted to end my life, knowing what I did to my daughter. The only thing that kept me from doing so was what she said to me; if I ended mine, I would have ended hers, too. That hurt me even more. Even knowing God forgave me, I still fought with myself, not willing to accept forgiveness so easily.

"When I realised how alone I was and that if I didn't forgive myself, I would never be good enough to face my daughter again. Forgiveness would force me to embrace God's mercy."

George turned to look at Sara and saw love in her eyes, and he smiled. "I love you so much, Pumpkin, and I'm sorry I hurt you so badly." Tears came uncontrollably.

Sara stroked the back of his hand. "Dad, it's okay . . ."

"Mr. Anderson, although I will not get into details with you about my past, I can assure you that I, too, felt undeserving of God's mercies. It took a while for me to accept it, so I am not one to cast a stone against you or anyone. We all have sinned, and God loved us enough to die for us all."

"Dad," Sara imputed, getting him to face her again. "Brady is the only one that knows; don't worry. He's the only person I trust. Brady has been a tower of strength for me, Dad, and I . . . I love him," she told him so both could hear.

"Sara?" Brady breathed, stunned, his heart beating fast.

She turned her gaze to him with a glow on her face.

"Say it again," he whispered, wanting to ensure he heard right.

Her heart danced, and her cheeks reddened. "I love you, Brady."

Forgetting that George sat in the room with them, Brady cupped Sara's cheeks and stared into her eyes. He knew she had spoken from her heart; very softly, he pressed his lips against hers and kissed her. Once the kiss broke, he pulled her into his arms and held her tight, savouring the moment.

"I love you, too, Sara," Brady cooed when he eased from their embrace and stared into her eyes. "I can't even put it in words, but you already know what's in my heart. You have helped me get past the darkest part of my life with the light within you. How could I not love you, baby?" He smiled, took a deep breath, and added, "Tell me, when did you know?"

Sara giggled. "When you held me outside to strengthen me before I faced Dad. I knew then that you would always be there for me and that you want me to be free of the past."

Without warning, Brady pulled her back into another kiss, forcing her to release George's hand and wrap it around him.

While George sat, watching them, he remembered the love he felt for his wife. Seeing his pumpkin found someone right for her, he felt relieved that she wouldn't be alone if he didn't make it.

He interjected by clearing his throat to get their attention. They looked at him and chuckled to themselves, causing him to join in.

CHAPTER 26- RESTORATION AND A DEEPER CONNECTION

After Sara made dinner and they ate, Brady asked them to join hands to pray for George's surgery to go well. He had seen the power of prayer through his grandmother, whose faith and persistence never wavered, especially when she stood fervently, praying for God's will to come to pass in his life. As they held hands, he closed his eyes and asked the Holy Spirit to guide him.

"Father, you are the beginning and the end. You said in your words that, 'you know the thoughts you have towards us, thoughts of peace and not of evil, to give us a future and hope. You said that when we call upon you and pray that you will listen.' Father, we stand here with George, who was once lost, but like Sara and I,

have now been found and have been washed and sanctified in the blood of your dear Son-Jesus, who is our precious Redeemer.

"Father, we asked that in the name of Jesus you will let your angels be in the operating room to guide the doctor's hands in George's surgery and deliver him from every incident and accidents that the devil may use to rob him of the long life that you promised him in Psalms 91:16. We ask you, Father, to cover both George and the entire operating team with the blood of Jesus and surround them with your consuming fire and destroy all the works of darkness that may arise.

"Father, you are the author and finisher of George's faith. We know that it is not your plan to cut his life short and rob him of enjoying the reunion with his daughter that they both have longed for. Therefore, we stand on your word that greater is he that is in George than he that is in the world. That You have already healed him internally and externally and of everything that would hinder your plans in his life, and all he needs to do now is to come in agreement with your word and receive it. We stand in agreement with George and ask that your will be done in his life. We thank you for a successful surgery tomorrow and give you all the praise now in Jesus' name. Amen."

"Amen," both Sara and George added.

That night, as Sara laid upon her bed, her mind was restless. She kept thinking about how she had managed to tell her dad that she loved Brady. She had wanted to tell Brady first—in a more romantic setting—so he would know how much she appreciated everything he had done for her.

A smile soon spread across her face as she remembered the look she saw on Brady's face when he heard her confess her love for him. She was happy to see her dad and knew how happy he was to see her. *It was all because of Brady,* and she loved him even more because of that. Sara took a deep breath, closed her eyes, and said her prayer. She soon drifted off to sleep with a smile on her face.

The next day, George handed Brady his car keys to drive them to the hospital. "You can use it to go wherever you wish while you are here in Charleston," he offered. After they arrived at the hospital, the doctors brought George to a room to prepare for the surgery. Just before the porter took him to the operating theatre, George gave Sara a hug and kissed her on her cheek, then shook Brady's hand. "Thank you for taking care of my daughter and for having a heart kind enough to accept me, even after what Sara told you about me."

"It was God's grace, George. I needed his mercy and forgiveness for all I did, too."

"It's time, Mr. Anderson," came the calm voice of the porter who stood by the door with a wheelchair.

George gave the porter a weak smile as he walked towards him. He glanced back at Sara and Brady before sitting in the chair and was driven out of the room.

Brady and Sara stood by the door and watched as the porter pushed him to the operating room.

Brady wrapped his arm around Sara's waist

at the sound of her sniffles.

"Don't worry, Sara. Trust God to do what He promised us in His words. Your dad will be fine."

"I do, Brady. It's just that I haven't seen him for a couple of years, and when I finally do, it's because of his surgery. I had wanted it to be in a better circumstance for both of us. I am proud of him, Brady, for turning his life around and staying the course. I just thought that when I returned home, it would be to introduce him to my fiancé and to ask him to walk me down the aisle at my wedding," she choked back tears.

"Let's go sit in the waiting area; it's going to take a while."

"Okay," Sara remarked and laid her head against Brady's shoulder as they walked over to the seating area in the waiting room.

As they sat, waiting, Brady let the things Sara told him marinated in his mind.

Am I ready for marriage? Will I be able to fulfil her every need and always keep her happy? I don't want to disappoint her like I did my mum and my dad.

Brady knew he loved her more than anyone and wanted to be with her forever. Her dad did not seem so bad either or even opposed to their relationship—not that he had any right to be. Brady sensed acceptance in the older man.

A couple of hours later, George came out of surgery. "All went well," the doctor in charge told them. "He'll be discharged in two days," he added and then further instructed them of everything they needed to do when George is released.

By the time George came home, Sara had already gone through the entire house and cleaned it for his recovery. Because he was used to being up and about at a certain time in the mornings for work, Sara had to be up to caution him.

"Dad, you know what the doctor said about getting out of bed so soon. You need a couple of day's bed rest to help heal properly," she told him and led him back to his bed.

One week after the surgery, George started moving about easier, free of the pain from the sutures and soreness. Having his daughter back home felt so special to him. The images that used to haunt him around the house when she was away were no more than a memory.

Brady could not help observing Sara's attitude towards her dad as she helped him get dressed, brought him his meals, and ensured he took his medication. She truly looked at ease with him.

Brady would often go up onto the roof to sketch images of the city and images he had stored in his memory of Sara and her dad together. He saw how much of a loving mother she would become while caring for her dad. At the end of that first week in Charleston, the tranquillity of the countryside called to him. He wondered—now that Sara and her dad were at peace with each other—would she want to go back with him. Was the love she felt for him strong enough that she would choose him over her dad and live with him wherever he chose?

"Brady," Sara called from behind him.

He turned his head around and smiled, watching her stroll towards him with a glass of orange juice and a broad smile on her face. She looked so radiant and beautiful. He scooted over on the bench, allowing her to sit next to him, and then took the glass of orange juice she outstretched to him.

"Can I see what you are drawing?" she asked as her eyes scanned over to the picture he was sketching.

"Sure," Brady handed her the sketchpad. He watched for her reaction, especially the ones he did of her and her dad. "What do you think of them?"

"Brady, you are very talented. You captured the emotions between my dad and me so well. Anyone who looks at them could see how we feel towards each other."

"Sara, I want to ask you something."

"Sure, ask me," she encouraged him.

"I know you love me, but now that your relationship is better with your dad, are you coming back home with me or are you going to stay here with him?"

Sara smiled. "Brady, you are my life now; how can I live anywhere you're not? I love my dad, but he is a mature man—able to handle himself. You brought back trust in my life and gave me love when I thought I wasn't meant to have it. Brady, I wanted to tell you I love you first, but I don't know how it just came out while talking to Dad. What I want to say, is that I don't see myself without you."

Brady placed the empty glass on the floor and took hold of her hands. "Will you marry me then, Sara? I can't promise you perfection, sometimes I may even disappoint you, but I won't love you less than what God puts in me to give you."

"Only you, Brady, and don't worry about disappointing me; you won't. It's the devil wanting you to think that. You have been nothing but supportive of me since we met. I guess I have gotten my wish after all in coming to see my dad. Now I can introduce him to my fiancé and ask him to walk me down the aisle, after all," she smiled and then kissed him.

"I guess everything worked out as how it was supposed to," Brady replied.

CHAPTER 27- BITTERSWEET GOODBYES

The following day, as Sara tended to George, Brady called Shawn before calling his dad and told them everything that had happened since leaving Lexington. Both were proud of him for getting through the worst and making progress, especially meeting Sara.

"I can't wait to meet her, Brady," Shawn chuckled into the phone.

Brady laughed. "You will love her."

"Denise and I miss you so much, Son, and we long to see you," Frank said, trying to sound tough when he heard Brady's voice on the other end.

"I'll come to visit you and let you meet Sara before we head back to Memphis, Dad. I have missed you both so much."

"Brady, I'm so sorry for the things I said to you when your mum passed away. For turning my back on you while you were in Lexington and taking so long to come to my senses," Frank said in a sombre tone. "I do love you, Son."

"Dad, it's okay. I love you, too. I know I put you through that, and I don't hold any grudges. Like God who chastises those he loves, I think you, turning from me then, forced me to look at where I wanted to be when I got out of Lexington. No more tears, okay, Dad? I am now writing a new and better chapter in my life, one with God's guidance, so smile."

"I love that, Son."

Later that night, as Brady and Sara sat on the rooftop, watching the sunset, a surge of excitement filled Brady. He was excited about seeing Shawn, his dad, and Denise again after so long and for them meeting Sara.

"Sara." He turned to her. "How would you feel about meeting my best friend Shawn, Denise, and my dad?"

Excitement surged through her. "Oh, Brady, I would like that very much!"

Brady pressed a kiss to her cheek. "I can't wait for you to meet them, . . . *but* how will you tell your dad we have to leave soon."

Sara thought for a moment. "Well, the doctor said a month is a sufficient amount of time for recovery, and Dad isn't one to just sit around when he starts to feel better. I bet you by next week, he'll be trying to get back into his workout routine." Sara laughed at the thought. "Could we stay for the month just to ensure that he heals properly, and then I'll tell him a couple of days before we leave?"

"Sure, we can do that."

"I think I'll wait until then to tell him we're getting married as well, just in case he gets all sappy thinking he won't see me again for a long time."

"A great idea."

Sara looped her hand through Brady's and rested her head on his shoulder. "Thank you so much for being so patient and understanding."

He kissed the top of her head and smile. "You are worth it, Sara."

****

George sat, staring absent-mindedly in front of the television a few days before Sara and Brady were to leave. He felt downcast. George was now fit to return to work the following month. His body was much stronger due to his workout routine, which he had started two and a half weeks after his surgery.

He had grown used to having his daughter around again. He had missed her face, her smile and just being able to watch her play the piano as she used to do for him. After seeing how much Brady cared for Sara and his firm Christian beliefs, George had also come to love him as a son. He knew Brady would be a good son-in-law.

Sara strolled into the living room, feeling blissful and froze when she noticed her dad's countenance. She sauntered over to the couch and sank next to him, averting his eyes off the television screen to her.

"Daddy, I want to ask you something." She reached for his hand and clasped it with hers.

"Anything, Pumpkin," George smiled.

A broad smile spread across Sara's face. "Brady and I are getting married, Daddy. Would you to walk me down the aisle?"

Tears welled up in George's eyes, "You have truly forgiven me, haven't you, Pumpkin?"

"Yes, Daddy, I have, and I love you, too."

"How could I not walk my baby girl down the aisle at her wedding, marrying a strong Christian man at that?" George wrapped his arms around her. "I love you, too, Pumpkin."

"Did I miss something?" Brady asked, walking into the living room with a chuckle.

"No, I just told Daddy about us getting married," Sara informed him.

George stood up, walked towards Brady, and extended his hand. "God could have never chosen a better man for my daughter than you, Brady. The Lord just brought her back to me, and for that, I am grateful. I will miss her not being here with me, but I know with you, she will be safe and loved, and I know she will love you just as much. Congratulations and welcome to the family, Son."

"Thank you, George," Brady responded with a smile.

****

George opened his arms towards Sara and smiled as all three stood at the bus terminal, waiting for the bus to arrive. Sara smiled, taking a deep breath and walked into his embrace. "I miss you already, Pumpkin," he whispered near her ear.

"I have always missed you, Daddy, and I'll be calling you every Friday from now on, okay? Try not to overdo your exercises for at least the next six months, alright?" she encouraged.

"Alright, Pumpkin, I promise," George squeezed her a little tighter.

Brady watched them with a smile on his face. He felt joy seeing the restoration of love between them.

George turned to Brady the moment he released Sara from his embrace and extended his hand. Brady gripped his hand firmly.

"Thank you for everything you have done for my daughter, Brady—for seeing beyond the exterior, allowing God to use you to restore joy into her life and bringing her back into mine." He exhaled.

"God also restored joy in me through her, George. She's a bigger blessing to me than I think I am to her."

"Not true," Sara interjected, laughing.

"Well, either way, I thank God for bringing us together." He chuckled. "Goodbye, for now, George, and take care of yourself."

George nodded and pointed behind them. "Here comes your bus."

"Goodbye, Daddy," Sara added before she looped her arm through Brady's and walked away.

"Heavenly Father, cover them under the precious blood of Jesus and take them safely to Miami," George prayed as he waved to them.

"Sara, we need to get our passports sorted out when we get home. I can't handle another trip like this if we have to travel again anytime soon," Brady told Sara once they were aboard the bus.

"I agree."

They slept, then woke up to eat, then slept again before the bus pulled into the station in Miami.

CHAPTER 28- HAPPY TIMES

Brady's heart thumped when the bus pulled into the station. He glanced through the window to see Shawn pacing about as nervously as how he felt. Brady turned his attention to Sara, gripped her hand, and with a deep breath, he smiled.

"Are you ready to meet everyone?"

"Are you ready?" she said, turning it back on him.

"It's been over nine years since I've seen them, but yes, I'm ready."

"And I'm here to support you as you were with dad and me." Sara smiled back at him.

"I know I have your support, Sara, and it's a blessing for me to have it, especially now having to face my dad."

"Do you see anyone out there?"

"Just Shawn; he's standing in front of the door and seems to be rushing everyone off to see if we're on." Brady chuckled.

"Let's go then and ease his anxiety."

Water saturated Brady's eyes as he descended the bus's steps and stared into Shawn's. Shawn let out a deep breath, smiled through watery eyes, then pulled Brady into a tight embrace. Their tears flowed.

Sara stepped off the bus and stood aside, allowing the two friends to have their moment. When they stepped back, both wiped their tears away with the back of their hands, then burst into laughter. This caused Sara to smile, feeling the joy in the air.

Brady turned to Sara, extended his hand to her, and pulled her to his side when she took his hand. "Shawn, this is Sara, my fiancé. Sara, this is Shawn, my best friend and brother."

"It's nice to meet you, Shawn," Sara replied, extending her hand towards him.

Shawn stared at Sara's extended hand, but instead of accepting it, he opened his arms for an embrace.

Sara stared up at Brady, who smiled at her. "He's a hugger."

Sara giggled and stepped into Shawn's embrace.

"It's so nice to meet you, Sara," Shawn spoke against her ear.

"There they are, Denise!" Frank's voice boomed in the background, averting Shawn, Sara, and Brady's eyes in his direction.

He and Denise ran towards them.

"Dad, Denise!" Brady dashed towards them.

"Brady!" Frank scurried, matching Brady's pace with Denise trying to keep up behind him.

Both men were in tears the minute their arms wrapped around each other.

"Give me a chance to hug him, too, Frank," Denise said as she caught up with them, causing them to laugh.

Brady loosened his grip around his dad's neck and pulled Denise into a tight squeeze and kissed her on both cheeks.

"I'm so glad to see you, Brady," Denise sobbed against his shoulder.

"I'm glad to see you, too," he whispered in her ear before letting her go.

With a smile on his face, Brady spun around to see Shawn and Sara walking towards them. He scampered towards them and reached for Sara's hand; her eyes danced when Brady entwined their fingers and pulled her close.

"Dad, Denise, this is my fiancé, Sara. Sara, meet my dad and Denise."

"Nice to meet you, Sara," both said, offering her hugs one after the other.

Shawn came and stood next to Brady while Sara hugged Frank and Denise. He rested a hand on Brady's shoulder and whispered, "She's pretty, Brady; you did well."

"I did, didn't I?" Brady whispered back with a smirk.

"Yes, you did brother."

"Let's go home, Son," Frank interrupted.

"Okay, Dad." Brady turned to Shawn again. "Tell Marie I'm coming for dinner tomorrow and bringing my fiancé to meet her."

Shawn smirked. "She will love that. She's been anxious to see you, too."

"Great. Come pick us up tomorrow, okay?"

"No problem."

Both embraced again before they parted for the night.

Sara loved Denise. The moment they got to Brady's parent's house, Denise took to her like a daughter and invited her into the kitchen to help her prepare dinner, giving Brady and his dad some time alone.

Denise put the bowl of potatoes into the sink, turned the tap on, and washed them off.

"Sara, could you peel these potatoes for me then cut them into cubes? I'll get started on browning the beef for the stew."

"Sure," Sara walked towards her at the sink. She washed her hands, took the bowl from Denise, and reached for a small knife. "What's this dish called?"

"It's a traditional Irish beef stew."

Denise pulled a frying pan from the cupboard and walked over to the stove. She turned the burner on and placed the pan on it. Then she poured some olive oil in and waited until the oil got hot before adding the beef chunks.

"We have a similar Jamaican dish, but we call it stew beef instead of beef stew and ours is not an entire meal on its own. It's more just the meat portion of the meal—usually served with rice."

"Isn't it amazing that even though we are of different cultures, we have so much in common still?"

Sara nodded and smiled.

"So, Sara, Brady told me you are of mixed heritage, part of which is Spanish."

"Yes, my mum is half Venezuelan and half Jamaican." She gathered all the potato peels and tossed them in the trash bag beneath the sink, then washed her hands again before she started cutting the potatoes into cubes.

"My mum had Spanish blood, too. I remember some of the Spanish dishes she taught me. Sometimes, I prepare them for Frank, and he loves most of them," she giggled.

Sara smiled. Being in the kitchen with Denise brought back good memories of her and her mum. "I remember all of those my mum taught me, even though I was a teen back then. I had to cook for me and my dad after she passed so I had to remember everything—both Spanish and Jamaican dishes."

"I only had one Jamaican dish—ackee and saltfish with fried dumplings, and it was good." Denise removed the browned beef from the pan, added more, and stirred.

"Where did you have that?" Sara stared at her, curious.

"Frank and I went on a Caribbean cruise many years ago to celebrate our 7th anniversary. It was served for breakfast a few mornings, and we made sure we never missed the days they served it."

Both laughed.

"I've finished cutting these up. What else can I assist you with?"

"Well, I'm just going to sauté this beef with some garlic, add the beef broth, water, Guinness stout, and then let it cook for an hour. Why don't you find out if Frank and Brady need anything to drink, and we can join them for an hour while the stew cooks?"

"I'll be back in a bit."

"Thank you, Lord, for sending Sara to love and care for my Brady," Denise prayed in her mind as she watched Sara walk out the kitchen door.

She never got to have any kids of her own, but the moment she met Brady, she loved him as her own. That love grew even more when he came to Miami to get over his drug addiction. She remembered how hard he tried to overcome it and the look on his face when he knew his dad was proud of him for completing the programme.

It broke her heart watching his demise, from losing his mum to getting discharged from the Navy to wandering the streets. She knew part of the reason he refused coming back to Miami was because of Frank. Her love for Brady almost cost her her marriage when she found out how many times he had reached out to Frank while in Lexington. Frank's stubbornness got to her at times.

It was she who got him to come to his senses. Now she sensed in Sara someone that would help Brady get through tough times if any more should come, and for that, she was happy.

Shawn arrived the next day at 5:00 p.m. When they got to his house and walked into the living room, Marie rushed towards Brady with tears in her eyes. She gave him a tight squeeze and pressed a kiss to both cheeks.

"I was so worried about you, Brady, when I heard you were living on the streets after leaving the Navy. I have prayed a lot for God to keep watch over you and to deliver you from all your troubles. Now I can see that He has. You look so strong and mature. I can see His light around you, too."

"Thank you for praying for me, Marie—I needed it." Brady reached for Sara's hand and pulled her close. "Marie, meet my fiancé, Sara," he added with a broad smile.

Marie's eyes sparkled, "Can I give you a hug, Sara?"

Sara nodded, stepped into Marie's embrace, and closed her eyes. She felt an overwhelming sense of gratitude to be so accepted by all of Brady's family and his closest friend.

After dinner, Sara offered to assist Marie with the cleaning up, leaving Brady and Shawn alone in the living room.

"Do you still think about your brother, John, a lot?" Shawn asked in a quiet tone.

Brady took a deep breath, "Not so much since Lexington. I felt like I disappointed him while I was there, knowing we had planned to serve our country together. I failed following through with doing it for both of us and then ending up on the other side of the law. Why do you ask such a question?"

Shawn leaned back into the sofa and stared up at the ceiling. "It's been over four years now since Mr. Jones died, and sometimes, I find myself thinking back to that day we met on the tracks. I was so desperate at that moment, not wanting to go back to my old ways, trying to believe in a God I hardly know. He was the only one who took a chance on me and allowed me to have a decent future. I miss him, Brady. He loved me like a father loves his son."

Brady placed his hand on Shawn's shoulder and squeezed. "It will get better. Although you will never forget, but the pain, guilt, or disappointed feelings do go away, and you heal—more so when you have support around you."

"I'll visit you, Brady, as soon as I have some free time from the farm."

"I would love that, Shawn."

"How have you been doing financially? Do you still have enough left from what your grandmother left you?"

"You want to take care of me, too, Shawn?" Brady smirked.

"You're my brother; of course I will help you until you get on your feet. It was tough for me to get a job as a teen out of St Peter's. What will it be like for you when those employers know you had an anger problem? Even with the prison wards and the guard's recommendations, it may take a while until God sends someone like Mr. Jones to help you."

"Shawn, I have been managing the money Grams left me with care and have some left. I want to sell my paintings, and Sara seems ready to be around people again, so we'll be fine."

"Brady, . . . please promise me that if it gets too tough to get jobs or sell your paintings that you will let me help, okay?"

"I promise, Shawn."

CHAPTER 29- A STRANGER'S HOMECOMING

After two weeks in Miami, Brady and Sara arrived back in Memphis. Both were exhausted and rested for most of that day before getting back to the routine of their lives.

A few months after they had returned home, Sara formed a partnership with Mrs. Walsh to sell fresh baked goods to the stores in town. Besides music, Sara discovered that baking was something she loved as well.

She felt blessed to have met Mrs. Walsh who was happy to have company around and took time to teach her everything she knew before agreeing to the idea of them working together. They decided to do all their baking in Mrs. Walsh's kitchen to give Brady the peace he needed while he worked—also because Mrs. Walsh had a much bigger kitchen area.

It was now almost a year and two months

since Sara and Brady came to live in the country and six months into their engagement. They had set their wedding to be in the next two months.

Brady, by this time, had completed quite a lot more paintings, and from time to time, he would call different galleries, asking them to showcase his paintings. He had hoped hearing his journey and transformation would be an inspiration the curators would have welcomed. Instead, each time he mentioned Lexington Prison, the doors of rejection kept slamming in his face.

"Baby, remember the Lord said that 'when we walk in His statutes and keep His commandments; He will give us rain in due season.' Trust God and his timing. Just keep painting while you wait," Sara would always say to encourage him.

One evening, while he and Sara had dinner, she said, "Brady, Mrs. Walsh got a letter from her granddaughter, Clara, today."

He arched a brow, "Oh, yeah. Did Mrs. Walsh say anything?"

"Only that Clara's coming home soon."

"Hmmm, I wonder what could be the cause of her wanting to return," Brady said to himself.

"What do you mean?" Sara asked by the puzzled look she saw on his face.

"Ever since we've been kids, Clara has always talked about leaving here and seeing the world." Brady's mind pondered on what Mrs. Walsh had told him about Clara and her fiancé breaking off their engagement with no explanation, and he suspected that her return had something to do with it.

"I thought it would've been something horrible from the look on your face."

Brady laid his fork on his plate and gave Sara his full attention. "Clara has always been very bold and opinionated. It was the reason John was so taken by her. They were kindred spirits. Clara made everything fun," he chuckled. "The country never seemed enough for her, and that's why I was wondering why she would return."

"Maybe she now realised that city life isn't all she thought, and she missed home." Sara tipped the glass to her head and drank the last of her juice.

"Maybe," Brady remembered Clara was also a bit flirtatious and sneaky but didn't bother sharing that with Sara. In his mind, he thought maybe Clara had changed, and it wouldn't make sense to share things about her that might not be the same anymore. In doing so, he would only have caused Sara to react negatively to Clara for no reason. He hoped that her coming home was not going to be a burden on the old woman, whom he loved dearly like his own grandmother.

****

Within a week of Mrs. Walsh getting her letter, Clara arrived and was ecstatic to hear that Brady was living at his grandmother's house. She didn't even take the day to spend with her grandmother; instead, she ran straight over to Brady's and pounded on his door.

Sara opened it.

"Hi, I'm Clara," Clara beamed. "Are you Sara?"

"Yes, I am." Sara stepped aside and pulled

the door wide open. "Do you want to come in?"

"You bet. Is Brady around? I came to wish him and yourself a congratulations. Grandma told me about your engagement; I hope you don't mind."

"No, it's okay. Come on, let me get you something to drink. We don't have alcohol, though, just juice and water, or coffee if you like," Sara chuckled as she led Clara into the living room.

"*Ahhh*, yes, Grandma did say that he's now born-again. I guess you are as well, right?"

"Yes, I am, and we're happy," Sara replied politely.

"Well, I don't believe in all that religious stuff anymore—never did anything for me," Clara shared as she took a seat on the couch. "I'll have a glass of juice."

"I'll be right back." Sara exited the room, walked into the kitchen, and poured a glass of orange juice for Clara. As soon as she returned to the living room, she handed Clara the juice and then turned towards the door again. "I'll be right back—I'm going to find Brady."

Brady was in the backyard, watering his grandmother's roses. He never had what most people call a 'green thumb,' but he promised to care for the roses after she died as a way of keeping the memory of her close.

"Brady!" Sara called, startling him. "You wouldn't believe whose sitting in our living room."

"Let me guess—Clara," he said as if not surprised.

"Yes," Sara said, surprised by his answer.

"How'd you know?"

"Well, that's how she is. She doesn't give you a warning when she does anything."

"Alright, well, come on, she's waiting to see you." Sara grabbed hold of his hand and pulled him towards the door and into the house.

CHAPTER 30- IMPULSIVE CLARA

Brady followed Sara into the living room and was greeted by a very excited Clara. She rushed towards him, flung her arms around his neck, and hugged him tightly, causing Sara to burst out laughing.

"Wow, Brady, you've grown into a very muscular guy, must have been from all that hard work they gave you in Lexington. It suits you very nicely, though," she said, staring up into his face with a grin on her face.

Brady couldn't help but smile at her comment about Lexington. He remembered how she could never filter what comes out of her mouth as not to offend anyone.

"Clara, I thought you would have put a muzzle on that mouth of yours by now. How many black eyes have you gotten since you left home?" he chuckled as he stepped away from her and walked across the living room to take a seat on the couch.

Clara burst into laughter at Brady's question. "My dear Brady, without all your great counselling, I found it tough. It's like I always seem to remember the good advice you used to give me, right after my mouth slips out something I immediately regret. You know me, though, I don't say things to make people feel bad, but they never see it that way." She plopped down beside him on the couch, and Sara sat next to her. "Anyhow, I came to say congrats. Grandma told me about your engagement to Sara here. And being that I haven't seen you for sooooo long, I couldn't wait."

"Thank you, Clara," Brady smiled, turning his gaze to Sara, who smiled back at him. "I have found my beloved, and she doesn't mind that I got muscles from Lexington," he teased her.

Clara turned to Sara. "You know all about his time in that place?"

"Yes, he told me everything and even of his life before . . ."

"And you stayed?" She interrupted with wide eyes and raised brows. "I mean, don't get me wrong, Brady is my dear friend from childhood, and I know him better than a lot of people. But in your case, as his fiancé, most women aren't so understanding or even willing to find out why he was that way. They don't want a man with so much 'baggage,' as they like to say," she said with sincerity.

Turning her attention back to Brady, she placed her hand on his and told him, "I was so worried about you, Brady, when I heard you were in Lexington. Your grandma was always so strong, thinking all would turn out good for you. She was always so good at encouraging us, and I felt bad when she died while you were still there. I kept wondering how you would get through life after being in Lexington and not having your closest supportive family members around.

"But I now see her words came to past for you, since God gave you someone, Sara, who has accepted you with all your baggage." Clara raised her arms and wrapped them around both Brady and Sara, causing them both to smile.

"Clara, what happened to your fiancé?" Brady asked, causing her to withdraw her hands from around their necks, dimming her smile.

"I'm sorry, Brady, that's for another time. I am not ready to talk about that right now, and besides, I came over here to celebrate with you both, not to share sad stories."

"Okay, Clara, but I hope you still feel comfortable sharing things with me. I don't want to see you sad and miserable. You're one of the few friends I have. Hey, let's watch some old reruns of sitcoms we used to watch. Sara loves those, too," he suggested.

"Sure."

They watched reruns for quite a while until Clara got sleepy. She excused herself for the night and bid them a goodnight.

Three days had passed since Clara returned home. Sara and Mrs. Walsh stood in the kitchen, applying the final touches on some of the pastries they had baked for the day's delivery. Mrs. Walsh picked up one batch of pastries she had just glazed with strawberry topping, walked towards the oven, and opened the door.

"Mrs. Walsh!" Sara shrieked.

"Huh!" Mrs. Walsh jumped in fright and spun around to face Sara.

"What are you doing?" Sara stared, wide-eyed at the batch of pastries in her hand.

Mrs. Walsh looked down into her hands. "Oh, my dear, I thought that was the refrigerator," she sighed and placed the batch of pastries back on the kitchen counter.

Sara got up, walked around to her, and placed her hand on her shoulder, "I'll put them in the fridge. You go sit down and take a break."

After Sara placed the pastries into the refrigerator, she poured two glasses of lemonade and joined Mrs. Walsh at the table.

"Do you want to talk about what's bothering you, Mrs. Walsh? I have noticed how absent-minded you have been since Clara arrived."

"My dear, I'm just worried about her. She hasn't said one word about what happened to her with her fiancé back in Canada since her return." She sighed and took a sip of the lemonade.

"Doesn't she confide in you, Mrs. Walsh?"

"No, my dear, the only person she used to tell her secrets to was Brady . . ."

"Brady!" Sara said, almost choking on the last sip of lemonade. "Wasn't she in love with John? Why tell Brady instead of him?" she asked with a sting of jealousy.

"Yes, Sara, Brady. Although she loved John, Brady was the one she confided in. John knew his brother well enough not to get jealous when he saw them talking alone. Brady was just that type of person who was easy to share things with in confidence. And he sure kept Clara's secrets safe from everyone, even from John if she asked him to," Mrs. Walsh said and laughed.

"But didn't John feel hurt that she trusted Brady over him with what bothered her?"

"If it was anyone else, John would, but he knew he wasn't good at keeping secrets, so he trusted Brady to keep them for Clara. Brady was great at giving Clara good advice, too. Saved her from running home with another bloody nose, crying because she couldn't filter that mouth of hers. Don't know who she gets that from," Mrs. Walsh giggled.

"Oh, now I get why Brady mentioned her getting a muzzle for her mouth when she arrived the other day." Sara laughed.

"Sara, by any chance, has Brady mentioned anything to you about Clara?" Mrs. Walsh asked, straight-faced now.

"No, nothing about her and her fiancé; all he's mentioned was about her childhood adventures with his brother, John."

"That means it's something very bad, and she doesn't know how to tell him now that you are in the picture," Mrs. Walsh said, looking like she was trying to solve a puzzle.

"What do you mean?"

"Well, now that Brady's a Christian, Clara probably feels that whatever she tells him would not be kept just between them. She knows Brady well enough to know that he wouldn't keep secrets from you, now that you're his fiancé."

"Oh, I understand. I'll talk to Brady at dinner tonight about getting her to open up to him. I'll tell him it's okay to keep what she tells him a secret if he can help her get over what happened in Canada. But how do you know she still struggles with it? She seems quite normal to me."

"If she was over it, she would have told me about it already. Even you would know about it from her own mouth. She's just masking it very well, and I don't like it at all. Who knows what could be going on in her head from day to day," she lamented.

"Where is she now, by the way? I haven't seen her for the past two days now," Sara asked.

"I am not sure; she leaves the house straight after we have breakfast. Maybe she's over at your house, hanging out with Brady. She is usually not the type to just sit around, not doing anything. Since she's been back, I've asked her if she's home for good or just for a visit, but she brushes off the conversation by saying she hasn't decided yet. That I should just think of it as a vacation for now."

Soon, the phone rang, interrupting their conversation.

"Hello, Mr. Skyers. Yes, we will have your order ready to be delivered in the next hour as promised. What's that? . . . . You want to know if you can get an additional batch of pastries, also? Well, you are lucky that we always prepare extra for emergencies," she chuckled. "Okay, Sir, see you then." Mrs. Walsh concluded with the customer then hung the phone up and sighed.

"Don't tell me; I know. Our customers never seem to know exactly how much they want," Sara said, getting up to check the other batch in the oven.

"But isn't it good when they ask for more?" Mrs. Walsh smiled.

"Yes, it is," Sara chuckled as they got back to completing their tasks, resting the conversation for another time.

CHAPTER 31- THE MYSTERY

By the time Sara and Mrs. Walsh returned from their day's delivery, it was almost 5:30 p.m.

"Have a good evening, Mrs. Walsh," Sara waved as she rushed off to prepare dinner. She thought Brady must still be in his studio. *"Father, please open a door for Brady with a gallery opening soon and take away his anxieties, in Jesus's name,"* she prayed. She knew he was anxious to share them with the world, even the very dark ones.

Sara tuned the radio to one of her favourite stations—one that played classic Spanish ballads—and began to sing along. It was something her mum used to do every time she worked around the house. Sometimes when the music kicked up the beat, her mum would stop working and dance along, oftentimes cause Sara to burst into laughter. There were even quite a few times when her mum noticed her laughing, she would take hold of Sara's hands and dance with her. Sara smiled at the memory when she realised she was now dancing along to the song. Halfway into preparing the meal, she heard footsteps coming down the stairs.

Clara's head popped into the kitchen with a smile on her face. "Hey, Sara, didn't know you were back." She waltzed across the kitchen and leaned against the sink, watching Sara.

"Yeah, it was a super busy day today. A few customers called for additional pastries, then we had a flat tyre on our way back." Sara placed the chicken in the oven and then set the timer. "Have you been here long?"

"About an hour. I had forgotten how peaceful it was out here."

"You missed it, didn't you?" Sara smiled, and then lifted the rice pot lid to check on it.

"Yes, I did; having Grandma or you guys around is good enough for me. I have to go now, though; I promised Grandma I would help her with dinner today. Brady's still at work upstairs—that boy sure knows how to get lost in his work."

"I know what you mean," Sara giggled.

"Ever since we were kids, he always got so caught up in whatever he did, shutting out everyone around him, especially when it came to his drawings or paintings. When John and I called him to play games with us, we had to always hide his sketch pad," Clara chuckled.

"He was that bad, huh?"

"Sure was. The minute we decided to rest so we could play again later, he would want to go draw or paint something. Sometimes he'd get so mad when he couldn't find his sketch pad and chase us through the woods and down to the river until he'd eventually laugh and join us." She sighed deeply. "Anyways, see you later."

"You, too, Clara."

Sara smiled and shook her head, watching Clara walk out the door before she went back to finishing dinner. As soon as it was done, she ran upstairs to take a quick shower then went back downstairs to arrange the table to serve the meal.

It seemed like Brady always knew how to time her, knowing exactly when to come downstairs for dinner. He was always already showered and smelled so good, wearing cologne that she had come to love. When she asked him what it was called, he told her, 'Swiss Army'.

After sitting down and saying grace, Brady noticed that Sara wore a distracted look on her face while she ate. "Sara, what's wrong?" he asked.

"Huh? *Oh*, I'm sorry; I was just thinking about Clara. Her grandmother is really worried about her and knows something is not right, even though she acts like nothing is wrong."

"Don't worry about Clara; she's a tough girl, always has been. When she's ready to talk, she will—I know something's wrong, too."

"You do?" her brows raised.

"Yes. She's not her usual self around me, which is always talkative. And sometimes she would wrap her arm around my shoulder while she talks, which showed she was comfortable— but don't start getting jealous now," he told her, chuckling. "That's just how she was, and even John knew that about her. Maybe now that she's an adult, she has realised that it would be quite inappropriate to keep doing it. But there is no excuse for her being quiet when she is such a talkative person by nature. It feels so strange, having her sit and just watch me paint, barely saying a word. I can almost sense that she wants to say something but holds back. I think she fears I will tell you her secret, and she's right. I don't want to keep anything from you; that only gives room for Satan to invade our relationship and cause mishaps."

"Brady, can I make a suggestion?"

"Sure, Sara."

"Mrs. Walsh said the same thing, too—that maybe that's the reason Clara hasn't talked about it yet. I told Mrs. Walsh that I would suggest you try to get Clara to talk and let her know that I'm okay with you not telling me what happened to her. It's her life, and it doesn't concern me, but I want you to be able to help her figure out how to come to terms with whatever happened. Maybe after she gets past it and is comfortable, she will share with her grandmother—or me, even."

"That's a good idea, but are you sure you will be okay with not knowing what happened, or even having her share her secret with me?"

"Yes. I trust you, and you're the only one from what Mrs. Walsh said that she confides in. I think she needs someone to talk to about it."

"You are truly very special, Sara, and God made you just for me. I love you. I will try to talk to her when she comes over again."

"Wonderful."

The next day, neither Sara nor Brady could stay inside. It was one of those super hot Saturdays that made people think of picnics in the park or a day at the beach. They decided to take a basket of food and head down to the river to spend the day there. They had hoped that Clara would have seen the note they left on the front door and come join them by the river. But she never did, and they took the opportunity to enjoy being alone with each other.

"Are you ready to spend forever with me, Sara?" Brady asked Sara as he wrapped his arms around her in the water.

"Forever and ever," her eyes gleamed with anticipation. Sara planted a soft kiss on his lips. "Maybe you will get tired of me after a couple of years when you're a famous painter and have the attention of many beautiful women."

"Come on, Sara, you know better than to think such a silly thing. After all, you and I are perfect together; who can take your place? For me, it is only you, and real beauty isn't what we see on the outside—it comes from within. You help me shine, and to me, you're the most beautiful woman," he said in a softened tone. "What about when your music takes off, or are you content with the business you and Mrs. Walsh have?"

"I'm happy with things as they are, but if God wants me to play, too . . . then, you'll still be number one for me."

Each night before they went to their respective bedrooms, they prayed together. They wanted to build their spiritual lives and cover their relationship and all they wanted God to do in their lives with the blood of Jesus, against all the devil's schemes and setbacks. They often spent time reading the word together when they could or even before they prayed. It was important to them to have the Lord as the centre of their lives, after everything he brought them through, and also for bringing them together.

CHAPTER 32- SOLVING THE MYSTERY

Brady rose from his stool and ambled over to the window to refresh himself with some cool fresh air. The heat of the day had become unbearable for him to continue working. After about ten minutes, taking in the cool air, he spotted Clara walking up the trodden path, coming from the river's direction.

"Hmmm," he said to himself. "that's not like her to venture off anywhere by herself."

Brady waited to see if she would stop by so he could get a chance to find out why, but she didn't until the following day.

****

"That's a very good piece you're working on, Brady," Clara spoke over Brady's shoulder, almost giving him a scare.

"Darn it, Clara! Why do you like sneaking up on me?" he said, annoyed. "You almost cost me this painting."

"Sorry about that, but I never snuck up on you, even when we were teens," she responded nonchalantly. "You are just always so caught up in your paintings that you never hear me—or anyone else for that matter." Clara chuckled and stepped away from Brady, sauntering around the room, eyeing everything.

"How have you been, by the way?" Brady asked.

"I'm okay." Clara stopped in front of the half-opened storeroom's door when she glimpsed the covered paintings. "Can I see those?" she pointed to the collection leant against the wall in the corner.

Brady glanced in her direction, then returned his focus to the painting and continued to apply the finish touches. "In time, Clara—not now."

She stepped away from the door and walked back over to him. "Has Sara seen them?"

Brady sighed and paused for a moment to stare at her. "Yes, she has; she has seen all that I have done. Are you *jealous*, Clara?" he squinted his brows, very disturbed.

"*No*, Brady. It's just that I have known you longer and well enough. I know everything about your terrible past, even if you think I don't. Our grandmas always talked on our verandah about everything, and soon, they'd talk about your mum and you and then pray. So, I heard everything and still loved you as my friend—nothing changed. So, I don't see why you can't let me see them, that's all," she pouted, feeling rejected.

Brady put his brush down and took hold of her arm. "Come on, and stop acting like a spoilt little girl."

He pushed the door open and took the paintings out one by one. He removed the covers from each painting with great care and laid them out for her to see. When Clara saw them, her mouth fell open, and her eyes widened.

"Brady, do you know how gifted you are? Looking at these, I can almost feel what you felt, and it's like tears could burst from my eyelids at any moment. Hearing your grandma talk about everything you went through doesn't make one truly understand the pain you felt as much as these paintings do." She inhaled deeply, and tears welled up in her eyes.

Brady pulled her over to a seat and sat next to her.

"Clara, you know you can still tell me anything, don't you? I'm still your friend, and if you're worried about me telling Sara, you don't have to. She said whatever you need to share with me is just between us, and if you want to tell her later, then fine."

"Why would she even think anything's wrong in the first place to suggest that?" she asked, sounding agitated.

"Your Gram asked her if I told her anything about you. She thought you would have told me about what happened in Canada."

"*Oooh*, Grandma is always worrying. I feel bad for not telling her what happened, Brady, but it has been very hard for even me to accept. How can I tell her?"

"Is that why you went down the river

yesterday?"

"I didn't go by the river yesterday. I was by the graveyard . . ."

"Graveyard? You mean our familys' burial ground?"

"Yes, Brady, isn't it the only one around here?" she answered sarcastically.

"Yes, it is," he said and laughed at himself.

"But yes, that's why I went there. I was trying to figure out what could have caused it to happen."

"Tell me what happened, Clara," he asked softly.

Clara took a deep breath and rocked back and forth. "Brady, I don't know if you will even comprehend it if I tell you, seeing that you have been out of touch with the world for quite a while. I mean, what did I do wrong for him to do that to me?" She snivelled.

"Clara, *please.*"

"Brady, . . . I caught my fiancé in bed with his best friend. *A MAN!* Do you know how that feels? Then he confessed that he could not help it and did not know what came over him. He had been sleeping with both his friend and me for months. I got so angry, I smashed his head with the nearest vase in the room and left. The worst part is that I still love him."

Brady hugged her and let her cry her heart out. All the heaviness she had been carrying all this while finally poured out. He was not sure what advice he could give her after hearing something this abnormal and crazy. This was something he truly had to keep between them until she wanted anyone else to know about it.

All he could think of at that moment to say to her was, "Clara, no matter how painful it all is, please don't get bitter against God or against your fiancé. Give God a chance to turn things around for you. He has been after you for so long, but you have been so busy chasing the world that you took no notice of Him. I'm not saying this is His doing, but I'm just saying maybe it's time to look up."

Brady didn't know what was coming out of his mouth as he spoke to her. He just allowed the Lord to use him to say what He needed her to hear at that moment. He could feel the resistance in her while he talked about not being bitter, but he understood this wasn't something to get past easily.

The minute he released her from his embrace, he pulled her back into his arms a second time to prevent her from dwelling too much on it. He saw she was beginning to let the very thing, he warned her about to start creeping in.

"Come on, let's go sit by the river and take your mind off all this. It was always our place of refuge from our problems. Don't worry; I'm here for you through this and will be praying for you as well. Just help me pack the paintings back inside the storeroom."

Clara wiped her tears and helped Brady cover the paintings and placed them back into the storeroom. After which, Brady covered the one he was working on and followed behind Clara out of the room.

As they sat by the water's edge, resting their feet in the cool water, Clara started to smile.

"Brady, I feel a little better knowing that my dearest friend knows what troubles me and that I can lean on you through it. The weight of it was beginning to bear down on me. I wanted to tell you the minute I came home but didn't want to put you in a difficult situation with Sara. I'm glad she doesn't mind not knowing because I don't think I could go one more day keeping to myself. And at the same time, I am not ready for anyone else to know the terrible, shameful secret I'm keeping yet."

"Don't worry, Clara; we'll get through it together as we always did with everything else."

Brady leaned back on both his elbows while swinging his feet back and forth in the water. Clara sat with her ankles crossed and her arms wrapped around her knees. She burst out laughing when she saw a silly grin appear on Brady's face. Then playfully, she ran her hand slowly up and down his shirt and lifted the edge of his shirt, taking a peek at his bare abs. "Brady, you certainly do have nice muscles," she said just before removing her hand.

"Are you trying to flirt with me, Clara?"

Brady watched the expression on her face, trying to see if there was something more to her admiring his muscles and being impulsive as usual.

"Oh, come on, Brady, because I admire your well-developed abs, you think I am flirting with you? I can't deny that you've grown very handsome, but as impetuous as I may be at times, I was never known to be a two-timer, and you know it," she defended.

"You're right. I'm sorry, Clara. Can we pray

together before we head back?" Brady suggested to her.

"I'm sorry, Brady, but I don't feel like it would do any good. I hate the devil for robbing me of my love, and I don't believe in God any more for allowing it all to happen. He didn't think I was worth sparing such a horrible fate when he allowed it to happen." She lost her smile, leapt to her feet, and ran off.

"Clara, wait!" Brady yelled as he jumped up and ran after her.

****

That night, Brady found it hard to sleep after knowing everything Clara told him about her fiancé. On his knees, he prayed for her pain as if it were his.

"Father in heaven, whose love for us is unconditional and who comfort us better than any human can, I honour you with all my heart. Lord, as you never forsook me because my Gram interceded for me, I kneel here before you on behalf of Clara, who also belongs to you. Elohim, I ask you to forgive her of her sins, wrap your loving arms around her and take her pain away. Let her feel your presence to know You haven't forsaken her and that Your love is better than life.

"I know more than anyone how it is to be bitter and feel rejected, yet I came to feel and know Your love for me. Fill her, Father, with Your love and wash her of all unclean spirits that may have attached themselves to her through her fiancé with the blood of Jesus. Let the evil deposits transferred in her body from his be purged by the blood of Jesus and cleanse her of

all her sins. Deliver her from all the enemies that plague her. Save her soul and renew a right spirit within her that she may walk in your divine purpose for her here on earth for Your namesake. In Jesus's name, I pray. Amen."

The following day at breakfast, Brady told Sara that Clara had opened up to him.

"That's great," Sara smiled.

"Yes, it is; although I can't tell you anything yet, I'm asking you to keep her in prayers and ask God to deliver her from the spirit of bitterness and hatred. Oh, please don't say anything to Mrs. Walsh yet. Her emotions may be too much for her to be satisfied, knowing Clara has opened up and her not knowing. I don't need her plaguing me about it when I need to figure out how to help Clara through it first."

"I can do that."

"Thank you, Sara."

CHAPTER 33- RENEWED FRIENDSHIP

Three weeks to Brady and Sara's wedding, and an unexpected guest showed up at their front door, giving Sara a startling surprise.

"Is this how you treat your supposed best friend?"

Sara stared into tear-stained eyes, and immediately, hers welled up with tears.

"Jessica?" she croaked. Sara pulled Jessica into a tight embrace and pressed her cheek against Jessica's. "I'm so sorry, Jessica," she whispered against her ear.

After a long, tearful embrace, Sara stood back and stared into Jessica's eyes. She felt a sudden rush of excitement and smiled. "Come, let's go inside and sit out on the deck and talk."

Jessica nodded and reached for her hand luggage that rested in front of her.

"I'll carry that," Sara said and grabbed hold

of the bag.

Jessica giggled, "Lead the way then, sister."

As they reached the deck, Jessica walked over to the wooden rails and stared out at the scenery.

"Wow, it's so beautiful here, Sara," she smiled broadly. "Listen to the birds—I could get used to living in a place like this."

Sara placed Jessica's bag on one of the deck chairs and walked over to her. "I remember how much you loved nature. Why don't you have a seat and relax?—let me go get us something to drink. I'll be right back, okay?"

"And miss this view," Jessica giggled. "You go get the drinks, and I'll relax right here."

Sara laughed. "As you wish."

This deck and this background make the perfect place to have a small get-together with close friends and family or, better yet, a wedding reception—yes, perfect. Jessica thought to herself.

"You still love cranberry juice, right?" Sara walked back with two glasses and stretched one to her.

"You remembered?"

Sara nodded.

"Yes, it's still my favourite," she giggled and sipped. "*Mmmm*, cool and refreshing."

Sara drank some of hers and then arched a brow at Jessica from the curious stare she got.

"What happened to you, Sara?" Jessica asked in a low voice.

Sara took a deep breath, wondering how much of what happened to her should she share.

"Can we sit down? I don't think I can talk

about this standing up."

"Okay," Jessica looped her hand through Sara's, and they walked over to the chairs and sat down.

Sara shared everything she went through since she left Jessica's house that night back in Charleston, excluding what happened with her dad. She decided Brady was the only one she wanted to know that secret.

"Sara, you were always so strong. Look how happy you are now and not traumatised by the past anymore."

"God and Brady did that for me, Jessica. Did you go to college as you wanted?"

Jessica beamed, "Yes, I went to New York and studied meteorology, just as I said I would."

"You were always so obsessed with storms, tornadoes, earthquakes, and other elements of nature since we were in kindergarten," Sara chuckled. "I'm glad you fulfilled your dream, Jessica."

"Yes, and I have been doing well since I left college and started working. But since my friends discovered that I'm good at organising and planning events, they all got me to organise their weddings for them." Jessica sighed. "All those depressed me after a while and left me wondering when I will be a bride instead of a bridesmaid or a maid of honour," she said with a weak smile.

"Your time will come soon; just have patience and don't just jump into a relationship because you want to get married." Sara wrapped her arm around her. "Jessica, how did you find me?"

"Your dad. I was so surprised, too. Whenever

I went home to spend Christmas with my parents, I would stop by your house to get news of your whereabouts and got disappointed every time. I almost didn't stop by this year . . ."

"Why not?"

"I hated seeing the look on your dad's face each time I showed up asking about you. It was like he was expecting you to show up, too."

"But it's not Christmas yet, so what brought you back so soon this year?"

"One of my friends' fiancé is from West Virginia, and they wanted to get married there. I couldn't resist the urge. You should see the smile on your dad's face when I stood at his door. He could not even speak. He dragged me inside, wrote down your address on a scratch pad, and handed it to me before he caught his breath. Then he told me you were also getting married. I was ecstatic, but then I also felt sad again."

"Why?"

"'Cause I finally found you, and you were about to do the one thing I yearned to do myself. I had told my friends that I would not be another bridesmaid or maid of honour—no more weddings, period. It hurt too much. But knowing I was going to see you again, I wanted to see *you* of all people get married, and if possible—as a gift—do everything for your wedding," she smiled again.

Sara kissed her cheek, "I would love that very much, Jessica—thank you. I have missed you so much, but I didn't know how to reach out to you after how I left. It was even hard to do so with my dad. It would have been harder to do without Brady's support."

"I know you were very close to your mum, and losing her was devastating, but I couldn't figure out why you would leave your dad knowing he was a mess without her, too."

"I didn't want to, Jessica, but with both of us grieving, it was making things worse for both of us. I had to leave; I thought it was the best way for us to get a grip on life and come to terms with the loss." Sara said. It was the best answer she could give her.

Jessica sighed. "I felt so hurt, too, when you left, but when I went to see your dad the first time, the condition he was in and the look on his face when I mentioned your name turned that hurt into constant worrying. I looked everywhere we loved to go, and it's when I couldn't find you that I started visiting your dad, hoping you would be back. Christmas became very sad for me after you disappeared. Every time I went to see your dad, hoping you had returned and then leaving disappointed, it made sitting down with my own family quite sad. All I could think about was you and what you were doing."

Sara hugged Jessica, and a few teardrops slipped from her eyes. "I'm sorry I put you through all that, and I thank you for not giving up on me. I love you."

"You are my sister, Sara, and I love you, too. I could not give up on you, even if you did on me," she teased.

Sara wiped the tears away and smiled. "Come, let me introduce you to Brady. He's upstairs."

CHAPTER 34- WEDDING PREPARATIONS

The next morning Sara took Jessica over to Mrs. Walsh and introduced them.

"It's nice to meet you, Jessica," Mrs. Walsh said with a broad smile.

"The pleasure is mine, Mrs. Walsh," Jessica replied.

"She's going to help me organise the wedding," Sara added.

"That's wonderful, Jessica. Would you like to taste the cake I'm baking for the wedding?"

Jessica's eyes lit up. "I would certainly like that."

Mrs. Walsh giggled and pushed back her chair from the kitchen table. She walked over to the kitchen counter, withdrew three small plates from the cupboard, and cut three slices of cake.

"Let me help you with that," Sara rushed over to assist her.

'I can manage, Sara," Mrs. Walsh laughed.

Sara ignored her. She picked up two of the dishes, brought them over to the table, and placed one in front of Jessica, leaving Mrs. Walsh to carry the other. Sara then went back, poured three glasses of orange juice, and joined them back at the table.

"Mrs. Walsh, this is super delicious. *Oh my.* You have to bake this at my wedding, too—that's if I do get married," she smirked.

"Don't be so negative, Jessica; your day will come just as I told you before."

"Yes, Jessica, don't give up hope," Mrs. Walsh added.

"Mrs. Walsh, where did you learn to bake such a delicious cake? Was it passed down in your family? What's it called?"

Mrs. Walsh laughed, "I learned to bake this cake from my best friend in college, Cecelia. It was passed down in her family from one generation to the next since the slave days on the plantation in the south. *'It's the one thing that the whites cannot take from us,'* Cecelia would always tell me. She wanted to pass it down to her children, but she got so ill back in college and knowing she wasn't going to make it, she gave it to me and asked me to preserve it for her through my own family. I had seen her make it many times before but never knew the ingredients, as she kept it a secret. One thing she asked me to do was never reveal the name and ingredients to anyone except my child."

"I understand. It's a great story and something worth preserving."

"Yes, and Clara, my granddaughter will be

helping me bake it and get introduced to making it."

"Did someone call my name?" Clara said, waltzing into the kitchen.

"I was just telling Jessica here that you will be helping me bake the cake for Brady and Sara's wedding."

"*Oh*, the secret cake; is there any left for me?"

"Yes, I save for you and Brady on the counter over there," Mrs. Walsh told her.

Clara went and cut a slice of the cake and came back and joined the women.

"Clara, this is my friend, Jessica; she's helping with the wedding arrangements," Sara said.

"Nice to meet you, Jessica."

"You, too, Clara." Jessica smiled and stuffed her mouth with the last piece of cake. "Sara, can I talk to you for a couple of minutes before you and Mrs. Walsh get started on baking your orders? It's about the wedding."

"Oh, you can ask me here. We're all family here," Sara responded with a smile.

Jessica smiled back, "All right. Well, I was thinking that since you and Brady don't care for an extravagant wedding, seeing your guest list is so small, and you want to keep your expenses at a minimum, we can send email invites. Then call to confirm that everyone received it and that they are coming. What do you think?"

"Sounds good to me."

"I also think the deck at Brady's house would be perfect for hosting the reception with its view and space. All fifteen guests could easily be accommodated. We just need maybe like three tables: one long one for all the guests, one for you and Brady, and one for the cake."

"Wow, I couldn't have agreed with you more. It would be even more special for Brady and me knowing it's where we opened up to each other about ourselves." Sara beamed.

"It's a splendid idea," Mrs. Walsh and Clara said in agreement.

"When are you going to get your wedding dress, Sara?" Clara asked.

"In about two or three days. Why don't you come along with Jessica and me?—be the objective one."

"The what?"

"The objective one. You can help me pick out a nice dress. Otherwise, Jessica will pick one for me. She's been telling me since we were teens that I have poor taste in picking out fancy dresses."

Clara burst out laughing and slapped Jessica on the shoulder, causing her to laugh as well. "I like you, Jessica. Sara, you can count on me to help you pick out a beautiful dress."

"Great."

"Well, now that I have what I need, I will leave you ladies to your baking and go design a lovely invitation and then send them off to your guests." Jessica smiled and stood up.

"I'll walk you to the door," Clara offered and stood up as well.

"Thanks."

When Clara and Jessica walked out of the kitchen, Mrs. Walsh and Sara put on their aprons and got to work. Sara looked over the orders for the day and blew out a breath.

We have a lot of orders to fill today, Mrs. Walsh; we might have to employ Clara's assistance today. Do you think she will be up for it?"

"Here she comes. Let's ask her."

"Ask me what?"

"We need your help getting the orders ready for today. Can you help us?" Sara asked.

"I sure can," she laughed. "What do you want me to do?"

"Well, first, you need to put this apron on," Mrs. Walsh stretched one towards her.

As soon as Clara finished knotting the apron around her waist, Mrs. Walsh handed her an order receipt.

"Seven dozen pumpkin raisin muffins and one dozen apple pies." Clara read with arched brows. "You make this much each day between the two of you?"

"Well, yes, most days. Sara usually bakes the muffins, and I do the pies, and whoever finishes first puts the boxes together to start packaging them."

"Oh, okay. So, what do you want me to do with this?"

"Look in the cupboard behind you—top shelf; you will find all the folded boxes for the pies and muffins. Take out what you need and start fixing them to package the muffins and pies once they're done."

"That's it?"

"*Oh*, you need to take out twice as much for the muffins; it's six per box. When you're finished with that task, you can start greasing the muffin pans."

"Sure thing, Grandma," she smirked and headed for the cupboard.

After helping with packaging all the muffins and pies in boxes, then bringing them out to the car, Clara came and sat on the kitchen chair, letting out a loud sigh, making both Mrs. Walsh and Sara laugh.

"Hard work, Clara?" Mrs. Walsh teased.

"Hard indeed, Grandma," she chuckled.

"Okay, ladies, I'm going to take a nap before my bath. Thank you, Clara, for offering to go with Sara today and give an old lady the day off," Mrs. Walsh laughed. "But, Clara, *please* try to control that mouth of yours around the customers."

All three burst into laughter.

As soon as Mrs. Walsh left the room, Clara got up and walked over to Sara when she noticed pastry sauce on Sara's face. She used her finger to wipe it off and then licked it off her finger, causing Sara to look at her funny.

"What!"

"I sometimes think you're still a kid trapped in that body of yours, Clara," Sara giggled. She removed her apron and wiped the mess from her face to start getting ready to go deliver the goods into town. Some of her hair fell into her face.

"Hold it," Clara said and very tenderly lifted the loose hair, placing them behind Sara's ear and smiled as she stared at her.

"Thanks, Clara, let's go," Sara said, picking up the receipt book and leading the way out of the kitchen.

Later that evening, when they returned

home, Sara bid Clara goodnight and gingerly walked over to the house. She found Jessica in the living room talking on the telephone, so she didn't bother disturbing her but instead went into the kitchen and started dinner. She knew Brady was taking his shower by now since she had returned a little later than usual. And sure enough, halfway into preparing the meal, he came down to join her in the kitchen and greeted her with an embrace.

"Sara, do you want to go take your bath now? I can finish up till you return," he offered.

"Thanks, Brady," Sara smiled and ran off up the stairs.

A couple of minutes later, she returned to see him dishing out the meal and handing them over to Jessica, who had joined him in the kitchen. It was sure nice to have company at the house other than just hers and Brady's. It made her feel like a kid on Christmas day.

Jessica was full of adventures to share about her time in college and of all the different people she had met during her studies.

"I have a funny story to tell you both," she told them.

"Great," Brady and Sara laughed in unison.

"Well, in college, I met a guy. He was so charming, very smart and romantic. His entire attitude made him seem like royalty, and then he told me that he was a prince. I laughed at first, but then I saw someone always picking him up from school, looking like a bodyguard. I started to believe him. Soon, I noticed that other female students started taking an interest in him, and he loved it. I told him I wasn't one for all the drama and that he should go out with some of the women that were so into him all of a sudden. He acted like he didn't want to at first but got over it like the next day," she laughed. "You know what happened a few weeks later? One of the girls that were so enamoured with him being a prince wanted to know where he lived and followed the car that came for him every day. He had a nice house but no mansion. Later, it was told that he only shared a prince's name and thought that having a bit of money could pass him off as one. Most women left, just to show you how shallow we can be at times, but one stayed, and I think it knocked some sense into him afterwards, to just be himself."

They all laughed.

That night, Brady drifted off to sleep with a smile on his face as he listened to the girls talking in Sara's room. It's like they were having a sleepover.

CHAPTER 35- SURPRISE!

The following day, Clara took Jessica into town to the bridal shop to show her what they offered. Both ladies were pleased with what they saw. Later that evening, Jessica made plans with Brady and Sara to go back to the shop the following day to purchase their gown and tuxedo. Mrs. Walsh offered to call the customers and inform them that no orders would be filled that day.

The next day, Clara found it funny at the bridal shop, watching both Brady and Sara struggling to select something that suited them. Jessica's frustration grew, trying to get them to agree to any of her suggestions. In the end, Clara saved the day with something all four agreed upon.

They got back to Brady's house at around 1:00 p.m., and all gathered on the deck. Brady thought he could enjoy their company and relax, but the minute the women began to discuss flower arrangements for the deck and house, he excused himself. This wasn't something that interested him, and he wanted Sara to spend as much time with her best friend as possible. His heart warmed seeing Clara looking a bit like her old self again. She had been spending a lot of time with Sara and Jessica, and he thought that was what she needed to keep her mind from dwelling on the past.

By 2:00 p.m., there came a knock at the front door. Sara excused herself and dashed off to answer it. She was surprised when she opened it.

"Shhh," the person replied.

Sara smiled broadly and pointed to the stairs. "First door on your right."

The person gave her a quick peck on the cheek and dashed off towards the stairs. Sara's heart swelled with joy, and she walked back out on the deck and joined the other ladies. Brady, who had resumed working on a painting, did not hear the creak of the door nor anyone entering.

"Oh, my word!" came the voice that now stood directly behind Brady, almost frightening him.

"Clara, how many times . . . !" he blurted, just before he turned to realise that it wasn't her.

"Really, Brady. I know my voice sounds nothing like that of a woman," the young man started.

"Shawn!" he gasped and pulled his friend into a hug. "I'm sorry, Shawn," he chuckled, "but she always sneaks up on me. My mind was just preoccupied with this painting that I took no notice that the voice I heard was that of a man's. But what are you doing here now? You do remember that the wedding's not for another two and a half weeks, right?" he asked, surprised at his friend's sudden visit.

"I know the wedding's not until two and a half more weeks, but I felt the urge to come now. So, I decided to surprise you, but you have surprised me instead," he said as he walked past Brady and stood directly in front of the almost completed painting.

"You like it?" Brady searched his eyes for truth.

"I remember seeing a few of your earlier paintings while we were at St. Peter's and thought they were good. However, you have brought me to the brink of tears by seeing how you portrayed my mum and me during the visit that I took you along. I love it and so will my mum. You somehow have a gift to see what's inside a person's heart and bring it to life.

"Your painting shows so much light in her eyes. I would never have to doubt how much she loves me, just by looking at this. Save this one for me, okay. I will buy this one from you for my mum," Shawn remarked and then stepped away from the painting and surveyed the rest of the room.

"Want to see the rest of those I have done so far? It's quite a lot. I have been trying to get a gallery to showcase them but to no avail," he lamented. He led Shawn to the storeroom and started taking them out before Shawn came and assisted him in taking out the rest.

"Your grandmother was right to push you to

not give up on this gift, Brady. Do you know how many people's lives can be changed by seeing your transformation through these paintings? Don't worry about not having a gallery reply to you yet; just keep painting till the Lord opens that door. Only He knows the right time to have the world see them," Shawn encouraged him.

"That's what Sara keeps saying when I get discouraged—to cheer me up. She's such a blessing to me, Shawn. I am so thankful to God. I truly—at one time—thought that no one would want me, after all I did in my life. But I have come to realise that God has made someone for everyone, and all our ups and downs are part of the process to complement the other," he shared.

"You want to know something strange?" Shawn asked.

"What!" Brady's brow arched in curiosity.

"The Lord told me that I will meet my wife at your wedding, and the strangest thing He said was that I will have to fight for her . . . ."

"What? Fight," Brady interrupted.

"Yes, Brady fight. I thought it was strange, too, but I trust God and know that He gives us the best gifts even if someone else looks at them as trash. I have fought so much in my past for all the wrong reasons. Why not trust God now and fight for the right things," he said confidently, walking over to the window and staring out towards the river and the lovely landscape. "It's truly a beautiful view you have from up here, Brady. Is that the river you liked to talk about so much when we were at St. Peter's?"

Walking over to Shawn, Brady stared over his shoulders out the window. "Yes. It's my place of relaxation and reflection. Tomorrow, I'll take you for a swim. *Oh*, I almost forget, did you check into a hotel?"

"No, I came straight here from the airport."

"Hmmm, well, I can get you a nice room at my neighbour and dear friend's, Mrs. Walsh's. I don't want you to sleep on my couch for the time that you're here, okay? Don't worry, she will love the company. She never wants Sara or me to leave when we go to visit her. Now Sara is over there every weekday, and her granddaughter Clara is back, too, so she's happy. But having a man around would make her smile even more," he teased.

"Come on, Brady, you know I don't fuss about where I sleep," Shawn slapped him on the shoulder with a grin.

"Well, doesn't matter; you're my brother, and while you're visiting, you will be comfortable. Come on, let me go introduce you to the ladies downstairs. I know you must have rushed past them to come and sneak up on me," he chuckled as he pushed him out the room and followed after him.

"Brother, you know me too well," Shawn chuckled as they descended the stairs.

As the men walked into the kitchen, they saw Sara preparing dinner and noticed the other two ladies still out on the deck. Brady led Shawn out to the deck and began to introduce him to them.

"Ladies, I would like you to meet my best man and my best friend, Shawn, who couldn't wait for the day of the wedding to show up," Brady teased with a snicker, causing Shawn to join in laughing. "Shawn, meet Clara and Jessica. Clara's from next door, where you will be staying, and Jessica is Sara's best friend and who's staying here until the wedding."

"He's staying at our place?" Clara asked with a raised eyebrow.

"Yeah, you know your grandma would love the extra company," he replied, plopping down next to her on the couch while Shawn sat across from them.

"You're right; she would," Clara smiled, "ever since grandpa died and Mum and Dad decided to move to Canada, she's been quite lonely and then worse when your grandma died. She used to call us every day back in Canada. It's the reason I chose to come back here when you-know-what happened," she shared.

"What happened?" Shawn questioned.

"Nothing you need to concern yourself with. It's a secret between my friend, Brady and I," she answered, giving Brady a smug look.

Jessica excused herself to go help Sara with dinner while Clara conversed with Brady and Shawn.

"So, Shawn, you and Brady were cellmates, huh?" Clara asked, staring at him curiously.

"Huh?" Shawn answered, surprised by her question.

"Ohh, don't mind her, Shawn. I should have warned you about her. She has a tendency to speak first, then think later, and it usually lands her in hot water with others, but she means no harm." Brady explained while chuckling to get a funny face from Clara, which caused Shawn to burst into laughter after observing it.

"Well," she interjected again.

"Yes, Clara, we were cellmates for two whole nights, and boy was it unpleasant. I wouldn't want to go through that again."

"Then you both went to a juvenile facility? I know why Brady went there, but what's your excuse?" she badgered him, causing him to laugh at how daring she was.

"Well, I had a bad temper, too, but I used to draw weapons a lot because of my dad. But I will share that another time if you're still interested to know that much about me," he told her, almost flirting with her.

"Whooo," Brady teased.

"Oh, quit that, Brady, and don't even go there. I'm not interested in anyone right now," she replied, getting serious.

"You guys want to have dinner out there or in here?" Sara yelled from the kitchen.

"We'll come inside," Brady shouted back. "It's beginning to get a little chilly out here, isn't it?" he asked Clara and Shawn.

"Sure is."

"Yeah."

They went inside and joined Sara and Jessica at the dinner table. While they were enjoying the meal, Shawn, who was sitting next to Brady, whispered into his ear, "Brady, I know who she is."

Startled, Brady turned to him and ask, "What! Who?"

"Your friend, Clara," he replied.

"Oh, Shawn, I now know why the Lord told you that you have to be willing to fight. She has been through a terrible ordeal and has even turned her back on God, too. Sara and I have been praying for her to overcome all she suffered."

"It's okay, Brady. I'm not a quitter, and I have the Lord of Host in my corner, so I must have victory," he said as he stared at Clara and smiled, causing her to look at him, perplexed.

After dinner, Brady accompanied Shawn over to Mrs. Walsh while Clara walked alongside them. Once inside the house, he introduced Shawn to Mrs. Walsh, who smiled broadly when she shook his hand.

"Mrs. Walsh, you don't mind having him stay here till the wedding, do you?" Brady asked.

"Oh, come on, Brady. Don't be silly; you know better than to ask such a silly question, and he's your best friend, too."

"See, I told you she would love having you here. I'll see you tomorrow," he told Shawn. "Goodnight, Clara, goodnight, Mrs. Walsh," he added and left.

After Brady left, Mrs. Walsh turned to them. "Would you both like to join me for a nightcap? It's still quite early," she grinned.

"Sure," both agreed.

They all walked into the living room, and Clara sat across from Shawn while Mrs. Walsh went into the kitchen to get the coffee.

Shawn jumped to his feet and stepped towards Mrs. Walsh when he saw her reenter the living room with a tray in her hand. "Oh, let me help you with that, Mrs. Walsh." He reached for the tray from her hand before she could object.

"Oh, thank you, dear; you and Brady are much alike—such gentlemen," she said with a chuckle.

CHAPTER 36- SHAWN AND CLARA

"Will you quit staring at me like that?" Clara said to Shawn, getting very annoyed. "You have been staring at me since dinner at Brady's. I'm not interested in you like that. And if you already have any notion in your head that you might have a chance, forget it!"

Shawn continued smiling as he took a sip of his coffee. Mrs. Walsh sat, enjoying the show she was getting from the two. There hasn't been much excitement at the house other than that of her and Sara's baking sessions.

"Is there something you know that I don't?" Clara asked him.

Shawn put down his coffee cup on the little table that lay before them and stared her in the eyes. "Yes, and you want to know, don't you?" he smirked.

"Yes!" she stressed, "quit stalling and tell

me."

"Okay, since you won't stop badgering me about it. I came here this early before the wedding to meet you . . ."

"What? Are you crazy? You didn't even know me before you came here," she asked, confused.

Mrs. Walsh was so caught up that she forgot about her coffee, which she never usually let gets cold.

"You're my wife, Clara, and don't call me crazy again," he commanded, giving her a serious look. "The Lord revealed it to me while we were having dinner earlier."

Clara laughed aloud, mocking him. "Now I know you are seriously demented. I have no interest in marrying anyone, especially one who comes in, saying he got his info from God. The same God that turned his back on me when he saw how my relationship was going and did nothing to fix it," she blurted out at him.

"Do you ever think that He knew what He was doing when He allowed whatever happened to take place? Maybe He wanted to spare you from a worse fate down the road where you would not recover and in doing so has redirected your steps," he advised.

"Maybe you're right, but I'm not ready to believe that yet. I'm going to bed. Goodnight!" she told him as she got up. She started to leave the room and then turned around. "Goodnight, Grandma, see you tomorrow," Clara marched out of the room without looking back at Shawn.

Mrs. Walsh stretched her hand over to Shawn's, getting his attention. "Don't let what she says frighten you. She's just hurt from her breakup with her fiancé. Whatever happened, no one knows yet as she has managed to keep it tightly lid. Only Brady would be someone she trusts to tell, and I don't know if she has done so yet. He was always who she confided in as a child. If God gave you that revelation about you and her, I beg you not to give up on her. I truly believe God knew why he took her from the last relationship. And now has brought you all the way here to meet someone you never met and telling you that she is your wife," Mrs. Walsh encouraged him and got up from her seat. "Come on, Shawn, I'll show you where you'll be sleeping."

"Thanks for the encouragement, Mrs. Walsh."

The next day, Brady came by shortly after breakfast to take Shawn down to the river to indulge him in the coolness of the water. Neither men spared anytime when they arrived at the water's edge and, with haste, stripped out of their sandals and shirts, left in their shorts before they dived into the water.

Both men were highly competitive and always challenged each other while back at St. Peter's. Now as they swam next to each other, it was no different. After about an hour, they panted and climbed back on the wooden planks, trying to catch their breath. They reminisced about their days at St. Peter's.

"Hey, you remember Major Stalker?" Brady laughed.

"Who could forget her?" Shawn chuckled. "You know, even though we all thought she was so mean, she turned out to be such a nice lady. I mean . . . I look back and see how hard it must have been for her to deal with tough guys like us."

"True. I saw her differently after the day we taught those bullies a lesson, and remember, she did intervene for Ricky and me when we applied to the Navy."

"I often find myself going back to that day when we taught those bullies a lesson whenever I stand face to face with tough guys back home. I'd just start laughing, which usually causes them to think I'm crazy and ignore me."

"We were a little crazy, though, but thank God for having His hand upon us, even then. When you're young, sometimes it's hard to see clearly how damaging your recklessness can be to your future."

"The one good thing that came from my reckless life back then was meeting you, my brother." Shawn shared and stretched his hand for a handshake.

Brady shook his and laughed aloud. "I still have that scar from where you punched me in the ribs," he added with a grin and pointed to the spot.

"Oh, yeah," Shawn rebutted and pointed to his rib. "I got one, too, remember?"

They both burst into laughter.

Brady took a deep breath, and with a straight face, he asked, "Have you heard from Ricky?"

"I knew I had forgotten to tell you something when you and Sara came to Miami. He's been calling and asking about you since you left the Navy. I told him everything, and he wanted to come to get you as I did, but I told him you needed space to come to terms with everything on your own. Since you came to Miami some months ago, I hadn't heard from him, and when I called his base, they said he was out at sea, so I mailed him a letter, hoping he would get it and be able to come to your wedding."

"I would love for him to show up at my wedding, Shawn."

"Let's just pray God will work it out that way, Brady."

Fifteen minutes later, Clara's footsteps broke into their conversation.

"Brady," she huffed, pressing her hands on her knees, trying to catch her breath. "Sara needs your help up at the house."

Brady jumped to his feet and grabbed for his shirt. "Clara, can you keep Shawn company until I return?"

Clara frowned at the idea. "Why don't you take him with you? Sara might need both your help." She then turned to stare at Shawn, who chuckled at her response.

Brady pushed his feet into his sandals. "Oh, come on, Clara, you're wasting time. You rushed down here, which must mean it's something important Sara wants. You know my friend is visiting, and I want him to enjoy as much of this place as he can while he's here."

"Oh, alright," she sighed.

"See you in a bit, buddy, and thanks, Clara," Brady told her and gave her a peck on the cheek, which made her smile.

"Are you still interested in knowing about my life?" Shawn grinned, much to her annoyance, after Brady sprinted off.

"If you want to share, I won't stop you," she shrugged as if uninterested and sat down crossed-legged a little distance from him.

"Well, I got my anger issue from my dad and also my use of weapons. My dad was quite the man then. He was much taller and bulkier than me. I was no match for him with just my fist, so I had to draw weapons to keep him at bay from my mother. I am not proud of how I was, but it led me to meet my best friend, and it was at St. Peter's that I learned about how many troubled teens are out there. Brady had a harder time coming to terms with his struggles and had to end up in Lexington to change, but it was a little better for me. After I returned home and found out that the way we live our lives affected our future, I was forced to seek refuge in God, whom I only knew of through my aunt. She always quoted scriptures about changing and the consequences if I did not," he chuckled.

Although acting as if she was not interested, Clara intently listened, and Shawn noticed but didn't make her aware.

"When I turned my life over to Christ, He opened up a door for me, and I received favour from a very kind man. I was now able to work and help care for my mum and ease the burden off my dear aunt, my sole provider. My mum had received a stroke at the hands of my dad. Sorry, I forgot to mention that earlier. Are you bored yet?" he smirked.

"Keep going," she told him.

"Anyways, now that I was working, my mum started getting better. She's recovered from the stroke now," he smiled, "then the Lord dropped a bombshell on me."

Clara turned to face him as curiosity got the best of her causing Shawn to smile. "What was it?" she asked.

"He said it was time to get married, and boy was I scared. After seeing what happened to my mum, I didn't want to get married and was content with a job that kept me busy. I just kept thinking that I would somehow turn out like my dad and a fear came over me. The Spirit of the Lord had to remind me that, 'God did not give me a spirit of fear but of love, power, and a sound mind.' Since then, I had to remind myself that when I surrendered my life to God, I had also renounced every sinful part of my life that may have been transferred through my dad or from him.

"I had asked the Lord to forgive his sins as well. Therefore, I was now, as the Bible says, 'a new creation, old things have passed away and behold all things now become new.' Speaking those verses over and over began to strengthen my faith to believe that I am not my father but who the Lord had created me to be. With that, I told him I was ready and would happily accept whom he chose for me. I knew that he would give me someone that will be able to help me fulfil his plans in my life and lift me where I fall short," he concluded.

"You're done?" she asked, sounding a bit softer as she spoke.

"Yes," he responded and lay quietly against the wooden planks with his hands crossed behind his head, staring up at the sky.

Clara continued to stare at him, unsure of what to say. She liked his personality, as it reminded her a little of her playful self, but she kept thinking, why couldn't God just change the man she fell in love with? Rid him from having that terrible obsession and allow them to be happy and live happily ever after?

Within an hour, Brady came running back down to the river, much to Clara's relief, as she'd started to have mixed feelings towards Shawn. As soon as Brady approached them, she excused herself and dashed off, causing Shawn to smile.

Throughout the next couple of days, Shawn noticed Clara's behaviour that no one else did. She flirted with Brady every time and played it off as nothing but mere affection from childhood. Around Sara, she was ever so sensitive to Sara's needs. To Sara, she seemed like an affectionate sister. Still, Shawn saw something in her eyes that Sara didn't notice. He suspected that she was plagued by an evil spirit that probably had something to do with her ex. He knew he had to take action now.

CHAPTER 37- SHAWN ON THE BATTLEFIELD

Going into the second week since he arrived at Brady's, Shawn decided he needed to go on three-day fast to pray for Clara's deliverance from the devil's hold. He told Brady, but figured he needed to also inform Mrs. Walsh as to not offend her when he refused to eat for the next three days. His fast was strictly just fruit juice and water.

Each day, he would start his fast with reading from Psalms 35 and 91, then fellowship with the Lord with songs of worship before he got into prayers.

"Father, as I come into prayer now, I ask in repentance for forgiveness for my sins and Clara's. Lord, you said that she is the one you chose for me, but I must fight for her, so here I am on the battlefield, ready to face the enemies that are warring against her soul and our marriage. Cover me and Clara, Father, with the

blood of Jesus, and gird me with the strength to not relent until this enemy is defeated and destroyed. I ask you, Father, to wash Clara in the blood of Jesus of every evil influence that has come into her life through her past relationships.

"I command every evil hold over her life by sexual demons—that plague her with sexual confusion—to release her now. I command them to depart from her soul, spirit, and body now by the power in the blood of Jesus. Let every evil deposit that was transferred into her body by her past sexual relationships be flushed out now by the cleansing power in the blood of Jesus. Father, you said in your word that our bodies are your temple and that it should be kept holy—that if any man defiles it, you will destroy him. Father, I ask that you cleanse her body from the crown of her head to the soles of her feet and make it your temple. Destroy every evil spirit that wants to defile her. Cleanse her from the spirit of sexual perversion, bitterness, and hurt. Lead her back into your arms with true repentance and be jealous over her against every unclean spirit in Jesus's name. Amen."

Throughout the day, Shawn kept on worshipping God in songs and declaring: "Clara's body is the temple of the Lord. Let *every lustful and perverted spirit release her and be destroyed by the all-consuming power of the Almighty, who is a jealous and holy God. Father, as Jesus used a whip to chase out the gamblers out of your temple who defile your house, do the same to all unclean spirits that are defiling Clara's body, your temple. As you removed the scales from Saul's eyes and revealed yourself to him, let the veil over Clara's eyes, blinding her from the truth, fall off, so she will see she's my wife. Open her heart to feel the love you place in her for me as you have opened mine for her. Cleanse us with the blood of Jesus of every hindrance to your purpose in our lives and guide us through your Holy Spirit in being fruitful. Fill us with the wisdom and understanding in the knowledge of your will in all spiritual wisdom and understanding in Jesus' name."*

He kept it up throughout the day into the next. At the end of the second day, he asked Brady to join him for the final day of fasting to strengthen his prayers in breaking every evil hold over her life. Brady was only too happy to join him, if only to see Clara happy again and his best friend rejoicing in God's favour.

Both men spent the entire day together praying and worshipping under the shady trees on the burial ground to be away from distraction. Sara knew where they were and managed to keep everything in check while they were away.

By the end of the day, Shawn went to bed exhausted, and that night, he received a dream from the Lord. In his dream, he saw Clara in a room with a male on one side of her and a female on the other.

Both were kissing her, caressing her in a sexual matter. She was not resisting. Then he saw himself appear into the same room and shouted at them. "In the name of Jesus, *I command you incubus and succubus spirits to loose her and be consumed by the fire of God. Her body belongs to God. You will not defile it in Jesus's name. Be consumed by fire and die in*

Jesus's name." He shouted at them until fire consumed them and they vanished, then he ran to hug her.

The following morning, Shawn could not wait until midday to tell Brady the good news, when he and Brady usually go to the river to swim and hang out. He knocked on Brady's front door with such urgency that it made Sara too nervous to answer. "It's okay, Sara, go back to what you were doing. I'll deal with this," Brady then walked to the front door and swung it opened with force. "Shawn!"

"Sorry, I couldn't wait till later to tell you what the Lord revealed to me. Come on, let's go," he urged Brady with excitement.

"I haven't had breakfast yet, Shawn," Brady yawned.

"Got that covered," he responded, raising his hand that held up two bags. "Two chicken sandwiches and a banana in each—should keep us till lunch. Just go inside and ask Sara to make us some lunch later."

"Alright, be right back," Brady grinned.

The morning was cool as they sat, relaxing by the river, eating their sandwiches. Curiosity bit Brady. "Well, what's the revelation you received?"

"The Lord showed me that Clara was being plagued by both incubus and succubus demons, something that I had suspected before."

"You did, how?"

"Yes, she was flirting with both you and Sara, and neither of you saw it. Each of you took it as just normal affection, but I saw something else. The Lord also showed me victory in the dream, too, of me conquering them."

"That's great, Shawn. Soon, she will be herself again."

"Yes, and now I feel confident that, in no time, Clara will be my wife, especially with this new love growing in my heart for her, which I know is from the Lord."

Brady smiled. "I know that feeling, too, Shawn. My heart is filled with such love for Sara that I knew could come only from God, too. I only wish that Mum and Gram were here to meet the woman I am about to marry. Sometimes sadness comes over me, knowing they will never meet her, and I know they both would have loved her, seeing how easy Dad took to her."

"I know, Brady, but be at peace knowing that all they hoped for you are coming to pass. Let that put joy in your heart knowing they are smiling now."

"You're right, Shawn," Brady smiled in agreement. "I'm so glad you came early, Shawn. I needed my best friend to take my mind off painting, from thinking so much about getting a gallery to showcase them."

"I'm happy, too. I realised that working so much and not doing anything else began to drain me. It's probably why the Lord said it's time to get married." He chuckled, closed his eyes, and took a deep breath.

"God knows best, brother," Brady said and kicked off his boots. "Let's see if you can beat me today."

"You only beat me last time because I was out of practice," Shawn added as he, too, began to remove his boots. "We shall see who will have the last laugh today."

"We'll see." Brady chuckled.

Both men removed their shirts and stood at the water's edge.

"Ready?" Shawn asked.

Brady nodded and began to count. One, two, three . . . *Splash*!

****

Jessica wanted to enjoy the river's coolness, too, but didn't want to feel like an intruder by dropping in the men. Instead, she waited until Sara was back early from her deliveries one evening, and both went down to join the men.

As all four sat, relaxing, Sara noticed how Jessica flirted with Shawn, much to her delight. She thought they would make a good pair, but she also noticed Shawn did not seem too optimistic in pursuing anything. From what Sara observed, Shawn was only being nice. Jessica took it only to be that Shawn was just the shy type and was not hindered by it.

Later that night, as they sat out on the deck, Sara pulled Brady away from the deck for a while to give Jessica and Shawn time alone to see what she thought of Shawn's disinterest. She would later find out from Jessica what transpired. She hoped for the best, as she wanted her friend to be as happy as she was.

Brady acted clueless to Sara's action and played along. He did not want to tell her what he knew about Shawn's interest in Clara. But he thought maybe it was a good test for Shawn to face before all things came together for him and Clara. If Shawn truly could resist the temptation that the devil was now throwing at him, then he would know that he was truly victorious.

As Shawn and Jessica sat out on the deck, Shawn felt uneasy by Jessica's advances, but he did not want to hurt her feelings and outright reject her. He could tell that she was indeed a wonderful person, but he had now accepted that God had someone for everyone and had already accepted whom God had chosen for him. Even if she still was hesitant about a lot of things, he trusted God and waited.

"Shawn, how about you and I go out for a nice dinner alone before the wedding, since we'll be going back to our own lives after? We can see where things could take us," Jessica suggested with a smile as she ran her fingers along his arm.

Very calmly, Shawn took hold of her hand, placed it on the table in front of them, and replied. "Well, dinner sounds good, but I don't think I can indulge in such things now. I'm here for my friend, and I don't want to rob myself of spending as much time with him as I can. It has been a long while since we had time together as brothers."

"Well, the offer still stands if you change your mind," she smiled, trying to hide her disappointment.

That night, Sara waited for Jessica to spill what happened between her and Shawn, but Jessica didn't mention it in their chitchat. Sara wondered why he didn't seem interested in her friend.

Meanwhile, Clara softened around Shawn but gave him no hope that she was interested in marriage. However, she enjoyed hanging around him, much to his delight. She wasn't as flirtatious as before around Brady or Sara, and that pleased him as well. He, however, kept on praising God for victory, thanking him for what he revealed to him, waiting on its manifestation.

CHAPTER 38- CELEBRATION TIME

Before the wedding day arrived, everyone came to Brady's house. Sara's dad flew in on an evening flight while Brady's dad and Denise came in on a later flight. All arrived at a good time to enjoy drinks and barbeque ribs on the deck in the coolness of the evening.

Being the gracious host that she was, Sara found it hard to sit still, ensuring everyone was comfortable and content. She moved back and forth into the kitchen, making sure drinks were always available to everyone. Upon returning from the kitchen with a bottle of wine, she noticed her friend Jessica wore a detached expression on her face as she stood next to Mrs. Walsh and her dad.

Sara stood back and watched Jessica to see if she could figure out why she wasn't as festive as everyone else. She followed Jessica's gaze over to the grill, where Shawn prepared the barbeque ribs, chatting up a storm with Clara and Brady. Sara noticed that while Brady and Shawn conversed, Shawn would steal a glance at Clara every now and then, like a man in love. Clara didn't bother entertaining his little gestures.

Sara saw Jessica's faint smile slip from her face. She now realised that things hadn't gone how she had hoped they would for her friend and Shawn, from what she saw. She walked towards Jessica, almost startling her, and gave her a big hug, causing her to smile.

The night went well. Soon, Jessica was happy again. Sara distracted her to prevent anyone else from noticing.

"Oh! This is the most excitement I've had in a very long time," Mrs. Walsh said, getting everyone's attention. "I'm sorry I have to take my leave so early, but I'm not as young as the rest of you anymore. I need adequate sleep to look my best tomorrow," she concluded and then headed for the front door, causing everyone to chuckle.

A couple of minutes later, George kissed Sara on her cheek and smiled. "Pumpkin, I should be going as well. I want to be very alert in the morning to walk you down the aisle."

She nodded with a smile.

"Wait for us!" Frank said to George while reaching for Denise's hand. "Come on, sweetheart."

"Good night, everyone," Denise said, smiling and waving her free hand.

"See you all in the morning," Frank added with a smile.

There was a chorus of goodnights until

Frank, George, and Denise walked out the door. Sara and Jessica went to the living room to chill out for a bit before they, too, went off to bed, leaving Brady, Shawn, and Clara out on the deck, laughing and chatting away.

As the two women lay out on the couch, exhausted from a very long day, Sara stared at Jessica. Jessica sat up and stared back.

"What is it, Sara? Ask what you are so anxious to find out," she said as if she could read Sara's mind.

"I'm sorry, Jessica, but I saw how you looked today, watching Clara and Shawn at the grill. I had hoped you would have shared with me what happened the other day, but you said nothing. Tell me what happened, please," she pleaded.

"Ohhh, you want to know about that," Jessica answered with an unenthusiastic look. "Well, that one—*Shawn,* is not for me, Sara. Can you believe he chose over me," she pointed a finger to herself, *"Clara?* She isn't even interested in him the way that I am," she said, bitter.

"Shawn told me I'm beautiful, but relationships are not always about that. He said that when we say we walk with Christ, we must trust Him to provide His best for us. And if His best doesn't look so good on the outside to others, what's on the inside is perfectly crafted for us. That's what he believes in. He also said that God has someone out there for me, and it would be unfair for him to rob me of that when we were not made for each other."

Jessica took a deep breath and then continued. "He said that a relationship should not be rushed into by our fleshly desires but be seen as God's blessing to us. Quote, unquote: his exact words," she relayed, looking very defeated and hurt, then slumped back into the couch.

"I'm sorry, Jessica, but he's right about God choosing the right ones for us. It saves us from falling prey to so many of the devil's destructive schemes for us Christians who say we walk with Him. Yet, we sometimes find ourselves in conflict when trusting God to choose right for us when He is our creator.

"I know you're not saved yet, but it still applies to you, too, since you also grew up in church and know a lot about who God is. To trust that He's real and able to do what we read and know about Him. I know that you sometimes feel like everyone else is getting married around you, and time passes you by. Soon, you will be thirty, but God's time," she stressed, "is the best time. Come on," Sara smiled and wrapped her arm around Jessica's shoulder. "Let's go pray before bed and ask God to reveal to you who His choice for you is, and until then, just wait."

The moment Sara and Jessica's footsteps disappeared up the stairs, Clara stepped out of the shadows. She walked towards the front door, feeling undeserving. She had come into the kitchen taking in the remaining glasses that she, Brady, and Shawn had used and wanted to thank Sara for being a wonderful host.

She figured that Sara probably would be having a chat with Jessica, whom she noticed was not very talkative to her the whole night. When she did not see them in the kitchen she strolled towards the living room to see if they were there and when she heard Jessica speaking her name, she hid and listened. Curiosity held her captive, and she couldn't find the courage to invade their conversation.

Now, standing alone at the front door, she folded her arms and thought to herself. *Why would Shawn be so determined to make me his wife? Is he as devoted to whatever God says that he doesn't even consider that I might have a terrible secret, which might shun him from me? Look at how I have openly rejected him, . . . yet he turned down a beautiful, well-accomplished woman for me. Well, I'm beautiful, too, not denying that—just battered and used.*

Clara stared up at the ceiling, "God, what could you have told Shawn about me that makes him want to fight for me so badly? Maybe I have been too hard-headed and unreasonable to accept that You might have protected me from something worst when You ripped me from Stanley."

"Hey, talking to yourself?" came a voice behind her. It was Shawn, "Ready to go, my love?" he smirked.

"Yes," she replied with softness in her eyes. Shawn stood, speechless for a few seconds, not used to this side of her.

Brady walked up to his two closest friends a few seconds later and wrapped his arms around Shawn's and Clara's shoulder. "Get some rest, you two. I need you both alert tomorrow."

Clara and Shawn both laughed.

"Goodnight, Brady," Clara tipped on her toes and pressed a kiss to his cheek. She opened the front door and stepped out and, after walking a few paces, turned around. "You coming?" she directed towards Shawn.

Shawn's lips curled into a smile, "Night, Brady," he tapped on Brady's back. "My wife calls."

"I heard," Brady chuckled. He closed the door behind Shawn, then took the stairs by two and headed for his bed, falling backwards and into a deep sleep.

****

Finally, it was the big day, and everyone was excited. Brady went ahead with Mrs. Walsh, Clara, and Shawn, leaving Sara to follow with Jessica. Both Brady's and Sara's parents met them at the church in town for the ceremony.

Sara stared at her reflection through her hand mirror as Jessica did her hair. A single tear escaped her eye. She sniffled.

"Sara," Jessica tilted her head.

Sara turned her head slightly to stare at Jessica. "Mmmm," she answered, trying to show her best smile.

"What's wrong? Is that a tear of joy or something else?"

Sara took a deep breath and patted the tear stain away. "It's a happy one. I just realised as I stare at myself how far I have come, knowing that God had someone for me that loves me past all of that after everything I endured. I just feel so blessed and grateful."

"You deserve to be happy, Sara; you're the nicest person I know, and Brady seems a good fit for you, too." Jessica finished pinning Sara's hair up and then sat down next to her. She sandwiched Sara's hand with hers and stared into her eyes. "Sara, I love you so much. You are my best friend and my sister. You and I have always encouraged each other with each other's best interest at heart. I thank you for what you said last night and for praying with me. I didn't really want to hear what you said about waiting and Shawn not being for me. But I knew you were saying what I needed to hear and not what I wanted, which is always the best thing.

"I will not let others make me feel bad if I'm not married at a certain age or to a certain type. But will wait until, in my heart, I feel that it's time and that it's the right person. I hope now that we have found each other again, being married will not keep you away from me. I know you have been writing music again and want to do more with what's inside you. And I believe that just as God will open that door soon for Brady, so will He for you as well, so keep creating, okay?"

Sara nodded, and Jessica hugged her with both getting emotional.

"*Ohh*, come on before you smear your makeup," Jessica teased.

Everyone gathered now in the church as Brady and Sara stood before the pastor, saying their vows.

"Do you take this man to be your lawfully wedded husband . . ." the pastor said. The church door squeaked open, averting everyone's attention to see a young man sneaking inside.

"Ricky!" Brady shouted and ran from the altar to give his friend an overly excited hug. Stepping back, both men stared at each other. Brady added, "I . . . I can't believe you're here!"

He choked on his words, remembering the disappointment he felt leaving Ricky alone in the Navy because he was medically unfit. "You got Shawn's letter?"

Ricky nodded. "Yes, I thought you would have gone back to Miami after the Navy, but when I called your folks and Shawn, they said you never came. I have been calling Shawn ever since to get news on your whereabouts. I wanted to come to get you myself and kick some sense in you, but Shawn convinced me you needed space to come to terms with everything. I hated it, but I understood. I love you, brother." They embraced again. "Congratulations, man."

The minister cleared his throat and smiled. "Are we going to have a wedding today?"

"Yes!" everyone in the church shouted.

Brady and Ricky laughed and briskly walked towards the altar. When they reached the second aisle, Brady stopped dead in his tracks. In the right aisle, he saw two faces that he did not take notice of before. He was so caught up with Sara's beautiful face. It was Shawn's mum, and aunt and both were smiling and looking so beautiful.

"Get back up there, Son," Frank told Brady.

"Yes, Sir," Brady laughed and rushed back to the altar and stood, facing Sara again.

"Now, where were we again?" the minister teased. "Ah, yes," he added. "Do you take this man to be your lawfully wedded husband?" he asked Sara.

Sara's eyes sparkled as she stared into Brady's. "I do."

"Do you," the pastor turned to Brady, "take this woman to be your lawfully wedded wife?"

"With all my heart, soul, and spirit," he smiled even bigger than her.

Everything else was a blur for them until the minister mentioned kissing the bride.

"I can certainly do that," Brady laughed, and everyone else joined.

"Well, go right ahead, Mr. O' Connor," the minister encouraged.

When Brady kissed his bride, it was almost as euphoric as the day he stepped out of Lexington and into freedom.

He and Sara felt as if their union was God healing them of their past, ushering them into a new life.

CHAPTER 39- NEWLYWEDS

The reception was going well on the house deck. They had rented a nice, long table to have all the guests sit on one side and reserved more room on the deck for dancing and also for better view and interaction with the bride and groom at their table.

Mrs. Walsh had gotten two friends of hers to serve the food and drinks to the wedding party. George and Frank beamed as they brought the double-layer cake Mrs. Walsh made for the couple and placed it on the table. As soon as the couple cut the cake, everyone cheered and snapped photos with their camera phones.

Ricky, who developed a love for films and photography, became the designated photographer for the wedding ceremony. He was honoured to do so. After the servers had taken the cake inside the kitchen to cut slices for everyone, they opened the dance floor.

"Can I have this dance?" Ricky asked Jessica after he put the camera down for a while.

A smile spread across her face. "You sure can," she allowed him to lead her to the dance area. "Thank you," she told him as they danced.

"What for?" he asked, a little puzzled.

She chuckled, blushing a little before she answered. "Well, you saved me from being the only young person not having a dance partner."

He laughed, "My pleasure."

Clara sat next to Shawn throughout the entire reception and was very reserved around him. It made him wonder if she had seen him the way he knew she would soon come to.

"Will you dance with me?" he heard her asked him.

Shawn stood up, stretched his hand towards her, and watched her slowly stand to her feet after placing her hand in his. Talkative as he usually was around her, Shawn now found himself speechless, uncertain as to what to say to her as they danced. He wanted to know so bad what was going through her mind but was afraid to ask. When the song ended, Clara held his hand and led him off the deck and into the living room.

"Shawn," she said, humbled, as they sat down on the couch. "I'm sorry for how I have been around you. I just couldn't see anyone for me other than Stanley, especially since he was always good to me. It was hard to let go, even with knowing about his other lifestyle. I just realised that there is more to your interest in me than physically—as I had thought. Your confidence and persistence in telling me that I am the one whom God chose for you, and then you rejecting Jessica who is very beautiful. I feel now that I need to let go of the past, step into the future, and give you a chance to be to me, the husband that God chose for me—that's if you still want me. But there is something about me I have to tell you first," she shared.

"Clara, I do want you, and I already know what you want to tell me. At least a summary of what the Lord revealed to me when I was on fasting," he began.

"Fasting. Why were you fasting?" Her brow arched curiously.

He smiled, raised his hand to her cheek, and caressed it, much to her surprise. The look he saw in her eyes, which were fixed on his, told him she was his.

"I did it for you. The Lord told me I had to fight, and after seeing how you kept rejecting me, I was not going to settle in defeat. I did what was needed to be done to gain your trust and your heart. It was then that the Lord showed me that you were being plagued by both a female and male sexual demon, which was why you had a desire for both female and male.

"I know it had something to do with your ex, but that's all the Lord revealed to me, and I have kept on praying since I saw victory in my dream from my fasting. You don't have to tell me anything else. Today is a day of new beginnings for us both, and just like how the Lord forgets our sins and remembers them no more, I want you to let the past be just that—the past. I accepted you as my woman because the Lord chose you for me, not by what I see with my eyes only. So, everything that you did before us is also the past."

Clara was blown away by his faith in God. Despite everything, he loved her and was willing to fight for her. How can she not strive to be devoted to such a man that she sees true Godly values in and commitment to the will of God? She leaned over and kissed his cheek just before the tears streamed down her face.

"Thank you for not giving up on me, even when the devil threw so many roadblocks your way. I am grateful for you wanting to share your heart with me, and I give you mine from this moment onwards," she whispered before she wiped her tears away.

"Will you marry me then, Clara?" Shawn asked.

"Yes, I will, and I will love you for the rest of my life. I'll always thank God for knowing what's best for me and bringing me home to receive his blessings for me," she added.

Brady took notice of them when they slipped away from the deck and smiled as he knew God was at work for his friend. He whispered to Sara what he suspected was happening. Although Sara was a bit disappointed that it wasn't in her best friend's favour, she was happy Clara was moving away from the past and embracing the future God planned for her.

Later that night, just before Shawn left the house with the others, he whispered to Brady the good news of his and Clara's engagement. Brady gave him a well-deserved hug and congrats.

Now, finally alone, both he and Sara stood at

the front door, watching their friends and family drive away, leaving them to the stillness of the night.

Brady turned his attention to his beautiful bride, "Sara," he whispered.

Sara stared up into his eyes and smiled.

"I love you so much," he told her.

Sara's eyes sparkled. "I love you, too . . . husband."

Brady kissed the top of her head. His heart pounded like beating drums from his anxiousness of wanting to take her into his arms and make love to her. He took a deep breath, then reached for her hand and placed it against his heart with his eyes fixed on hers.

Almost like a trance, they held each other's gazes as Brady proceeded to walk backwards, leading Sara up the stairs to his bedroom—now theirs. As soon as they entered the room, he caressed her cheeks with the back of his hand before cupping them, drawing her in for a deep and tender kiss.

Sara felt cherished with each of Brady's kisses, and they overwhelmed her. Uncontrollable tears streamed down her face, and with one finger, Brady wiped them from her cheeks. He kissed her forehead and placed another tender kiss on her lips.

"*Sara*," Brady drew her eyes to his, "see me . . . and no one else, okay?"

She nodded.

He reached for the straps of her dress and gently removed them from her shoulders, one by one. He needed her to feel safe with him to not associate their intimacy with her past horrors.

As the dress slipped from her shoulders, he kissed her neck and shoulder, causing her to quiver in delight.

Brady reached behind her, unhooked her bra, and let it fall to the floor. He then stood back and stared at her, stupefied at the woman that now belonged to him. "Sara, you are so beautiful."

Sara stepped out of her last piece of clothing, showing Brady she trusted him and wanted to be his, always. She reached for Brady's shirt and unbuttoned the first. "Let me do it," she said.

He smiled.

After removing his clothes, Brady scooped her in his arms and carried her to the bed.

"Brady," Sara whispered just before he lowered her to the bed.

"Hmmm, sweetheart?" Brady cooed.

"You have my heart forever. I love you so much. Let our hearts forever be entwined."

"Forever and ever, sweetheart; our hearts will be one."

They locked themselves in the house for three days, making love, discovering each other's bodies before anyone saw them again. By then, the rest of the wedding party was just about ready to go back home and came by to say their final goodbyes. Shawn announced to every one of his and Clara's engagements, which made everyone happy that soon another wedding will be in celebration.

CHAPTER 40- A SILVER LINING EMERGED

As life started to normalise for the newlyweds, Sara gave more time to writing songs as she found new inspiration since she and Brady tied the knot.

A month into their marriage, Brady felt compelled to visit Lexington. At first, he was hesitant, but after discussing it with Sara, he realised that God's hands were involved. When he stepped into the place he once hated, he felt a sense of purpose for being there.

Since then, he took on the role of a counsellor to help reform the hostile prisoners that found it hard to relate to anyone else. He felt nothing but fulfilment around them. All the terrible things that had happened in his life helped him connect with the prisoners. It gave him firm grounds to stand on in convincing them that everything Satan meant for evil, God can and will if they'd allow him to turn around for their good. His greatest joy came when a prisoner asked him to pray for him and lead him to salvation.

Seeing him at work with the prisoners and them connecting with him had many guards dumbfounded to believe that it was the same Brady, whom many feared and hated at one time. They saw so much joy and peace pouring out of him when he was with the prisoners. Even as he conversed with them, seeing the two paintings that he donated to the prison convinced them he was truly a changed man.

Four months into his and Sara's marriage, Brady felt blessed in more ways than he thought he deserved: a beautiful wife, who loved him even knowing everything about his past, being a mentor to prisoners who struggled with difficulties as he once did, building a solid relationship with his dad again, and seeing his best friend Shawn tie the knot with his other dear friend, Clara.

At the sixth month mark of their marriage, Brady felt hope surge through him, time and time again. He knew God was about to open a door for his paintings to be showcased, and he kept giving thanks.

One Friday afternoon, after completing his latest painting, he stepped outside and began to water his grandmother's roses. He smiled, picturing the surprised look on Sara's face when she sees the painting he'd just finished. It was a surprise for her, and he marvelled how he managed to keep it a secret from her.

"Brady!" Sara said as she rushed into the backyard, jumping up and down.

"What is it?" Brady's eyes widened in anticipation.

"Telephone call for you, sweetheart—it's a gallery!"

"A gallery?" he replied, shocked.

"Yes, hurry up!" She grabbed his hand and dragged him into the living room.

Brady picked up the receiver and took a deep breath. "Hello, this is Mr. O'Connor."

"Good afternoon, Mr. O'Connor. I have very good news for you. But first, I want to apologise to you on behalf of myself and my partner, Mr. James, for taking so long to get back to you. We had so many things going on and had to have all those dealt with. Now back to the reason I called. Are you still interested in us displaying your artwork? It would be an honour for us. Your pieces are truly inspiring and reflect so much heart and emotion—something many painters lack these days. I have been looking for someone whose work connects with people's lives and hearts for so long, and the minute Mr. James and I viewed samples of your work, we were in love. So will you give us the honour? Oh, by the way, I'm Mrs. Mason," she finished with a laugh as excitement filled her voice.

Brady stood, speechless as he listened to Mrs. Mason speak while Sara stared at him with apprehension.

"Brady! Snap out of it. Say something, honey," Sara whispered.

"Yes . . . yes! Thank you so much, Mrs. Mason, for the offer. I would be happy having your gallery exhibit my work," he laughed. "*Oh, by the way, when will the exhibition be held?*"

"Mr. James and I think one month from today would be good; it gives us sufficient time to do all the publicity needed to make your show a great success. Let's say on the 22nd of May at 6:00 p.m."

"That's fine with me, Mrs. Mason."

"Wonderful. I'll have my secretary email you all we need to do and finalise for next month's exhibition. Have a great day, Mr. O'Connor, and thank you for giving us this opportunity. You will not regret it."

Brady hung up the phone, swooped Sara up in his arms, and spun her around, "It's happening, Sara," he laughed ecstatically and kissed her.

Sara laughed in excitement, too. "We have to go tell Mrs. Walsh!" she added.

"Yes, of course! Let's go."

After sharing the news with Mrs. Walsh, who proposed to make them dinner, Sara and Brady could not contain their excitement. They called everyone and told them the news and informed them to expect an invitation email soon. Everyone agreed that they would not miss the event for anything.

****

Brady's nervousness and excitement elevated as the exhibit date drew closer. Sara found it comforting to soothe his worries with tender massages or playing him a love song she wrote for him. Those always made him feel special, eased his nervousness, and restored confidence just in time for the exhibition.

The gallery was only two hours away, and this made Brady and Sara happy. By the time they arrived, both were stunned at the size of the crowd walking into the gallery. Mrs. Mason stood at the entrance, waiting for them. When she saw them approaching, she ran towards them and greeted them with a broad smile. She led them inside and introduced them to Mr. James and other important persons contributing to the gallery show. Soon, they saw their friends and family, greeted them, and introduced them to Mrs. Mason and Mr. James.

Mrs. Mason excused herself and went to commence the show. "Good evening, everyone. Welcome to tonight's show, where all the pieces you see are done by a very special person who paints with such heart and emotion. I know many of you have already connected with some of his work. However, before introducing him to you and having him share something about his inspiration behind his work, we have one special performance from an upcoming artist with great talent. Please help me welcome Mrs. Sara O' Connor." Mrs. Mason concluded, the crowd clapping.

Brady gave Sara a surprised look just before she ran off, smiling. She sat at the piano and turned her gaze to him, then she opened her mouth and began to sing as she played. His heart felt overwhelmed as he listened to the words she sang to him.

In my heart, I know I am yours.
In my spirit, I have no doubt.
All my life, I have longed to feel a love like yours.
Now here you are, and I have been healed

*from a heart of
sorrow and brokenness.*
2
*God be praised for choosing you and
strengthening me to trust in you.
Although my eyes could not see or my heart
could feel that you were the one when I met you.
God's love in me helped me to accept and
love you as the one He made just for me.
I will forever give him honour and glorify his
name for giving me His best gift in you.*

Brady found it hard to stand strong after listening to Sara and hide it with a smile. After her performance, Mrs. Mason took the mic again, and getting everyone's attention again, she began.

"I hope you all enjoyed that performance. Isn't she just lovely, and when I introduce our guest speaker, you will understand the connection," she shared with a laugh. "Well, without further ado, please welcome Mr. Brady O' Connor."

Everyone cheered and laughed, now realising that Sara was his wife.

Brady took a few quick strides to reach Mrs. Mason and smiled graciously when she handed him the microphone. His eyes scanned the room, and finally, it landed on Sara, whose smile spoke something to him that no one else understood.

"Good evening, everyone," he began softly and then took a deep breath. "Thank you all for coming and celebrating with me and sharing in with my entire work and life's journey." His voice grew louder and sounded more confident. "I want to first give God thanks for helping me to find myself and also for blessing me with a beautiful wife, who is my joy and my best friend. She has been such a blessing in my life, and I love her dearly." He smiled at Sara, and everyone's eyes followed his gaze. They all smiled as if they, too, felt what he felt. They turned their gazes back to him again when he continued his speech.

"Now let me get your attention to the paintings, and as you can see, I have arranged them into two categories; Darkness and Light. This section, which I have called Darkness, was originally ten pieces and was all about me, as you can see by most. Painting them helped me release everything inside me that I wanted to forget. Once I painted them, I felt free from the pain of it all. The others in this section I did of my friend's sufferings as well. I have made this arrangement to show you the contrast of how darkness and light work together.

"The Bible says in Genesis that, 'in the beginning, the earth was void and darkness was upon the face of the deep. Then the Lord said let there be light, and there was light.' I said this to show you that out of the darkness came light. Now this section that I call into the light, you can see the difference, and these came out of me when I started walking in God's light.

"I allowed him to transform my life and show me meaning. There should be no one that says his or her life is too dark to have any light in it. The word of God just proved that everyone who is in darkness also has light. We just have to want to step out into it for God to shine through us. No one in the world is pure light, only Jesus Christ is, and that is why he is called the Light of the world.

"I am sorry if I sound like a preacher, and I don't mean to be, but for you to understand my collection, you have to truly understand the connection between the light and darkness that we face each day and where God fits in.

"From all I endured in life, I could have chosen to stay in darkness, as could all my friends here, but where would we be? None would be happy or have joy and peace—only hate, bitterness, and sorrow.

"The devil likes to tell people that they are too far gone to be saved when he knows that's not true, but if he can get you to believe that, then he has done his job. Once we remember that all of us have darkness in us, but that there is also light, this is why people do good sometimes, even a bad person, hope is there for us to have Christ shine his greater light in us—flood out the darkness.

"This is my work, yes, but I want to introduce you to three persons very dear to me, who you also see in some of these paintings. Sara, Shawn, and Clara, could you guys come here for a minute, please? Look at them; they all look happy now, but if they share what they've been through, you might not believe them, but with God's grace and mercy, all endured and conquered.

"Our lives here on earth aren't just to live for ourselves and enjoy all the worldly things we see. Our lives are to love all with the love of Christ, who died for all, so we can be free from all the sorrow darkness brings. Only evil loves darkness—what will you choose? Thank you all, and God bless."

CHAPTER 41 - PASSING THE TEST

The entire gallery was completely silent while Brady spoke. This was not what they were used to in attending an exhibition, and it took them a good few minutes before they started clapping at the end of his speech.

Listening to him attribute the transformation in his life to God, whose guidance helped him and his friends find peace from their tragic past, made the audience look into their own lives, wondering if they were truly happy. It had them thinking that there's more to life than all the worldly things that most had come to see as normal.

Although Brady felt nervous talking the way he did, he found that he couldn't stop when he started. Inside, he felt that the message he was sharing was more important than his painting sales, and he continued. He felt proud as he stood there feeling like his life had contributed some good; even if it's this small thing to others, he was happy. The God, he trusted, would always provide a way for him to flourish in life, even if from something small.

The night seemed a success; even at the end, Mrs. Mason and Mr. James felt proud by his words, which didn't aim to gain riches for himself but to share something he received with others.

Sara took Brady's hand and led him away from the crowd to a quiet spot. She took two glasses of champagne from a passing waiter and offered one to Brady before she gave him her full attention.

"Honey, I have one final surprise for you, and this I know you will be very pleased with," she began piquing his curiosity.

"Sara, you have surprised me already tonight by that song. How much more can you give me, sweetheart?" he asked as he caressed her cheek.

Shortly after they had slipped away from everyone, Shawn and Clara realised they were missing as they had some great news to share with them. They didn't want to share it over the phone. As they scanned the gallery, they soon caught sight of them in a corner, talking alone, and tried sneaking up on them. However, as soon as they heard Sara telling Brady that she had another surprise, they decided to play like sneaky kids and listened first before they disrupted them with their news.

"Brady, we are going to have a baby!" they heard Sara announced to Brady just before he took her into his arms, celebrating.

"So are we!" announced Shawn and Clara, at the same time as they stepped out of their hiding spot, almost frightening Brady and Sara before they all burst into laughter.

"What?" Brady exclaimed.

"You are?" Sara asked, surprised.

"Wow," said Brady and Sara, now excited for their friends. They all hugged and celebrated.

"Well, let's toast to God," Shawn said.

"Yes," everyone agreed as they raised their glasses.

"Who has taught all of us that everything the devil meant for evil in our lives, He has the power to turn around for our good, and we thank Him that He has done so for us. To our Lord and Saviour, Jesus Christ, we honour you and thank you for not letting go of us and for helping us find our way. Cheers," Brady said.

"Cheers," joined the others.

Finally, the world was getting to see Brady's paintings; the press had made sure of it. His speech caused many to start buzzing, but all in all, it turned out for good. Many persons bought his paintings and asked for another show soon. Some even came to him, seeking advice.

This opened his eyes to the extent of his influence in motivating and uplifting people beyond those in prison. Some of the money he made from his paintings he planned to help the homeless, who were in situations like he was.

For the next two months, none of the changes that came made him give less time to his marriage or his relationship with his creator. He knew what was most important. Brady was most excited about the new addition to his family.

The minute Sara's stomach started showing in her fourth month of pregnancy, Brady started feeling a sense of gratitude and truly favoured by God to be given such a gift. However, sadness crept up on him each time he looked at his beautiful wife and picturing her holding their child or each time he kissed her belly.

Memories of his grandmother, Ruth, kept on flashing before him. He remembered how she'd fill albums with his and John's baby photos from their first visit, and she never stopped until John had died and Brady stopped visiting.

She always said special prayers for them, declaring God's blessings for them, and it pained him that she would not be there to do the same for his baby when he came. However, after a few days, he smiled again, knowing in his heart she would be pleased, that he had fulfilled her wishes.

After breakfast one morning, he went down to the rosebush and picked a nice bunch. He then strolled down to the burial ground and placed them on his grandmother's grave.

"You were right, Gram. I now see God's hand in my life and my paintings. He told me once to paint away from the darkness and bury them, and the light will come. It has, Gram, but I no longer want to throw away the dark ones if they can help others see that even in their dark lives, light is there, hiding, just waiting to be released. I miss your wisdom and your smile, and more than anything, I wanted you to see my firstborn." He took a deep breath, and a tear escaped his eye. "I know you will always be a part of my life.

"Thank you for not giving up on me, even

when I gave up on myself, and for always praying for me. Sometimes we don't see the life that God has set for us because of all the roadblocks or disasters we meet. Not knowing that, even though they may make us uncomfortable or hurt, God is still with us along the way. And His hands, ensuring that we don't die before we fulfil our purpose. This is why he makes people like you, Gram, who stands faithfully in praying for us until we start to see clearly; until we trust in His divine plan. Don't worry about Dad; he's super excited that he's getting grandkids, and I will make sure he's alright. I love you, sweet Gram."

"Brady!" Sara's voice boomed through the cemetery.

Spinning around, he spotted her walking towards him, looking worried.

"Why didn't you tell me you were coming here, hun? I would have come with you," she asked him as she approached him.

"I'm sorry, sweetheart, I just wasn't thinking clearly. I just wanted Gram to know I miss her and how I wished she was around to see that what she prayed for me has come to pass. Even mum and John, I now miss, seeing that everything has turned around for me." Brady wrapped his arms around her and hugged her tight. "I love you so much, Sara."

"I love you even more, Brady." Stepping out of his embrace, Sara smiled. "Let's go home—just know that your gram, your mum, and John are all happy now that you have found your way. All they ever wanted for you was for you to be happy."

"And *that* I am, baby. I really am."

Brady extended his arm to her. She looped hers through his and off they went to live the rest of their lives, knowing God was with them.

The End

A Word From The Author

ENJOYED THIS BOOK? YOU CAN MAKE A BIG DIFFERENCE.

REVIEWS ARE VITAL FOR AN AUTHOR. THEY CAN INCREASE EXPOSURE for my books, invite other readers to discover my stories, and have an impact on the quality of marketing I can access to promote my work. I do not have the funds to take out full-page ads in newspapers or put up posters on the subway, unlike major publishers. But I desire to have something else which is more powerful than money, and that is a committed and enthusiastic group of readers.

If you've enjoyed this story, then I would be super grateful if you could spend a few minutes, leaving an honest review on the book's page. You can jump right to the page by going to either of the links below.

Life's Journey our Greatest Test (Amazon)
https://www.amazon.com/dp/B09HRD157Q

Life's Journey our Greatest Test (Kobo)
https://bit.ly/3wkVlgU

Life's Journey our Greatest Test (Goodreads)
https://bit.ly/3wjJhfM

Life's Journey our Greatest Test (Bookbub)
https://bit.ly/2ZWUh6R

OTHER AVAILABLE BOOKS BY THE AUTHOR

- Predestined Love
- The Path of the Chosen Warriors
- A Shattered Life Restored
- Her Treasured love

Books can be purchased at any of these online stores.

Amazon link:
https://www.amazon.com/Marshalee-Patterson/e/B0917Z7DDH/

Kobo stores link:
https://store.kobobooks.com/search?Query=marshalee+patterson

Building a relationship with my readers is very important to me. I have discovered that God provided me with this form of ministry to share Him with the world.

For those interested in learning how I imagined the characters and the story itself, direct your questions to any link below. I am eager to get to know those who enjoy my books and welcome your interaction. I eagerly await the impact the stories had on you. Thank you for all your support, especially those of you who encourage others to purchase a copy. I am sincerely grateful for you all.

This is why I am building a mailing list. I send out occasional no-spam newsletters with previews of upcoming releases, special offers, exclusive giveaways, and author updates.

Please sign up at:

https://marshaleepatterson1.wixsite.com/christianbooks

Did you enjoy this book and would like your review to be showcase on my website reader's review page? Then email me your review along with a picture of you holding the book to: marshaleepattersonbooks3@gmail.com

You can also follow me on my YouTube channel and listen to free audio samples of all my books: https://www.youtube.com/@marshaleepatterson

THE SINNER'S PRAYERS

Dear Jesus,
Your word in 1 John 1v9 says that, "If we confess our sins, You are faithful and just to forgive us our sins, and to cleanse us from all unrighteousness." I acknowledge that I am a sinner and that I have sinned against you. Have mercy on me, Oh Lord, and forgive me for all my sins. I turn my back on my sins now and I renounce every association and every covenant with the kingdom of darkness. I repent also for the sins of my parents and all my ancestors. I ask you, Lord Jesus, to break every curse that has been passed down to me and my family through our bloodline because of our parents and our ancestor's unrepented sins, and covenants they may have formed with the kingdom of darkness. Your word also says in Romans 10v9, "That if thou shalt confess with thy mouth the Lord Jesus, and shalt believe in thine heart that God hath raised him from the dead, thou shalt be saved." Lord Jesus, I believe that You died on the cross for me and that God the Father raised You on the third day. I now surrender my life and my will to your purpose for me here on earth and thank you for sending the Holy –Spirit who will come and dwell inside of me, sealing me to the Father, and who will guide me into my divine destiny. Lord Jesus, please come now into my heart and be my Saviour. Amen.

Thank you for reading my book/s. I decided to add this to my books after having a conversation with the Lord one day and felt the need to. If you felt the Lord speaking to you through any of the characters and want to give your life over to him, become part of the covenant we have with God. I invite you to pray the sinner's prayer above and then get into a church that not only teaches you about Jesus Christ, but one that teaches on Holiness, not feel-good sermons. I know I am a bit different from most Christian fiction authors, but I know that God wants to reach all and not many will go into a church because they might feel condemned but still have a desire to have a relationship with God and so, I hope that through my books, you will feel God speaking to you and giving you his love, hope, and healing through what you are going through. You are not alone; I have gone through most of what my characters have in one way or another. You can send me emails as well, if you sometimes need a word of encouragement or someone to pray with you

ABOUT THE AUTHOR

Marshalee Patterson was born in Kingston, Jamaica. She always had a love for reading. It was while attending Merl Grove High School that she discovered she loved writing stories. Some of her favourite novels were written by Charles Dickens and Victor Hugo, as she found she liked the true-to-life stories to which we all can relate.

Despite discovering her love for reading and writing, she pursued a banking career as a Bank Teller after leaving high school. Not until after she went to Italy in 2003 did she start reliving her experiences about which she wrote. She gives credit to being a Christian; it is the Holy Spirit that guides her in writing her books. Marshalee hopes that through her novels, she can inspire people of all ages with the message of hope in Christ, to show them that through Him comes deliverance.

With this medium, her goal is to supply readers with the knowledge of victoriously overcoming Satan's tactics. Creating these stories exposes the devices Satan uses and allows readers to better detect various situations in which demonic doors open. Through spiritual warfare prayers which have seen results, she hopes readers can learn from them to stand firm against the devil.

She is a lover of nature and its tranquillity. She finds nature refreshing and peaceful. She loves different cultures, especially the Spanish culture. A culture she strongly feels strengthens our ability to learn to appreciate where we have otherwise been ungrateful. She adores Salsa music dances, well, too. She is a proud Jamaican.

Made in United States
North Haven, CT
08 March 2023